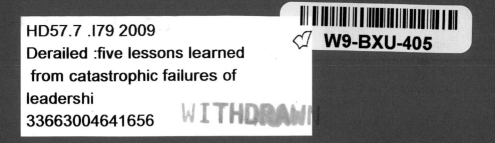
DATE DUE

Praise for *Derailed*

"CEOs are being scrutinized at this time in history like never before. This increased level of scrutiny is the direct result of a number of very public and expensive miscarriages of leadership. Irwin does a favor for CEOs and all leaders interested in navigating a more successful career by reminding us that extremely competent and capable people can "derail" when they ignore a disabling weakness, a blind spot or even a strength taken to an excess. We ALL have this innate potential to derail!"

—Carlos Sepulveda,
President & CEO, Interstate Batteries

"Most books on character are yawners, yet Tim Irwin's *Derailed* is a page-turner! In the hyper-competitive and intoxicating world of being a winner, where our strengths and success often drown out our ability to hear truth, we need to hear Irwin's voice. Packed with real stories of derailed giants, Irwin gives us the tools to ensure we can lead the pack while staying on track. *Derailed* is must-read for anyone who is or aspires to be a leader who stays on track."

—David W. Miller, Ph.D., Director,
Princeton University Faith & Work Initiative,
and President, The Avodah Institute

"The character principles outlined in Tim's new book Derailed are foundational to developing and sustaining great leadership in life and business. A must read for leaders or aspiring leaders at all levels. Tim presents these lessons in a way that allows the reader to relate with real life examples and the consequences that ensue when key principles are ignored."

—Michael L. Ducker, President,
FedEx Express International

"As someone who has worked with high performers my entire career Tim Irwin's book is a powerful tool. I have seen many successes and also many failures and Tim's four reasons for either success or failure are right on target. Tim emphasizes character, and humility is a close second. Whether in sports or business character and humility are usually the determining factors. I strongly recommend this powerful book not only to my friends, but anyone who wants a primer on how to succeed in life or business."

—*Dick Schultz, Executive Director,*
National Collegiate Athletic Association (ret),
Executive Director, United States Olympic Committee (ret)

"Derailed is a compelling, practical and readable book that will make you a better leader, a better person, and someone who can rise above."

—*Marshall Goldsmith, New York Times best-selling author of*
Succession: Are You Ready? *and*
What Got You Here Won't Get You There

"*Derailed—Five Lessons Learned from Catastrophic Failures of Leadership* is thought-provoking, and insightful. In it Tim Irwin skillfully examines several real-life case studies of leadership gone wrong. The author also artfully illustrates key principles to help those already in leadership, or those aspiring to it, avoid the pitfalls that can easily ensnare executives along the way to the top. Compelling and incisive, this is a great handbook on how to avoid those perils."

—*Mac McQuiston, President & CEO,*
The CEO Forum, Inc.

"Tim Irwin has done it again. First he gave us valuable insights on keys to meeting challenges in *Run with the Bulls without*

Getting Trampled. Now in *Derailed,* he shares equally important thoughts on the other side of the coin-how to avoid critical
mistakes in leadership. I have had the great experience of seeing
Tim Irwin's advice make a profound impact on an organization.
Derailed shares his insights on avoiding critical mistakes in leadership from the hard lessons of those who did make mistakes.
These are images the reader will not forget. Any reader will have
much to take to heart."

—*David Ripsom, President & CEO,*
Nuclear Electric Insurance Limited

"In my years as a corporate executive and now in the non-profit
world, I have observed many leaders fall by the wayside. Tim
Irwin is right. It's usually not about competence . . . it's about
character. *Derailed* is an outstanding resource for anyone in a
position of influence. Tim's message is compelling, and his lively
stories and real-world examples make this a wonderfully readable book."

—*Johanna C. Zeilstra, Co-Founder and Chief Operations Officer,*
Give Back, LLC

"This book is not only great, but it is also timely. Tim Irwin
takes ancient wisdom about character and brings it to bear on
the most up-to-date challenges facing leaders today. We all
ignore these lessons at our peril. I highly recommend this book."

—*Dr. Tim Keller, Senior Pastor,*
Redeemer Presbyterian Church, New York City

"Any effective leader needs their perspective challenged, *Derailed*
serves as this kind of challenge . . . a 'gut-check' reminding us of
our vulnerabilities and forcing us to validate our strength of
character. *Derailed* leverages the experiences of some very talented

leaders who may have lost their way to draw the reader to an assessment of their own character."

"Rarely does a book impact me both personally and professionally in such a profound way. *Derailed* by Dr. Tim Irwin did. This is a crucially important message that's really needed now. Irwin hits home with clarity about why so many leaders are failing. I want a lot of people to read this book because we need to stay on track."

"Dr Tim Irwin has nailed it in" *Derailed*!" It seems like almost every day we hear of yet another high profile corporate or government official or sports personality succumbing to a massive failure in judgment. Why is it that so many of these smart, competent and experienced individuals feel that the rules don't apply to them? Tim's discussion of the characteristics necessary to keep from "Derailing" will dramatically impact how you lead. The real life stories and examples in this book will provide you insights that are a must for staying on track."

"A must read for those in and for all who aspire to leadership. Shelves are full of how-to books listing various formulas of what-to-do for success. Missing is a closer look at what-not-to-do to avoid derailment! Irwin fills this vacuum with his analysis of corporate leadership failures. He's hit a home run identifying those primary pitfalls experienced by well known business leaders that resulted in their dismissal. We all can learn from this insightful study and copies should be required reading for all corporate officers."

—*Ron F. Wagley; Chairman, CEO, & President,*
Transamerica Insurance (ret)

"CEOs are the new royalty. Sometimes these anointed kings are generous, insightful and use their power wisely. Other times they fall prey to the same hubris and tone deafness that felled the kings in the golden ages. There are useful lessons here for everyone, crowned or not."

—*Seth Godin, Author,* Tribes

"Tim Irwin has provided in this book an early warning system for all individuals and companies seeking to avoid the very public types of disasters which have recently become so very prevalent. "Derailment" from this point forward can be predicted and most importantly avoided by leaders at all levels given this resource."

—*Lee B. Torrence,*
IBM Managing Director and Senior State Executive (Ret)

"Over the course of my career, I've observed many hundreds of leaders under the most stressful circumstances imaginable. Rarely does a book so effectively capture the truth about what makes some leaders great and others fail. *Derailed* is a compelling, practical and readable book that will make you a better leader and a better person,. Whether in business, the military, or in any other endeavor, if you aspire to leadership, this book is a must read!"

—*Patrick P. Caruana,*
Lieutenant General (Ret) United States Air Force

"We've seen what the world looks like with Leaders who believe their own press . . . Imagine a world where Leaders put their ego aside, and genuinely collaborate, empower, apologize and foster the human spirit in others. I'd like to live in that world, and Tim Irwin just may have the roadmap."

—*Nancy Ortberg,*
Author of Unleashing the Power of Rubber Bands: Lessons in Non-Linear Leadership

FIVE LESSONS
LEARNED FROM
CATASTROPHIC
FAILURES OF
LEADERSHIP

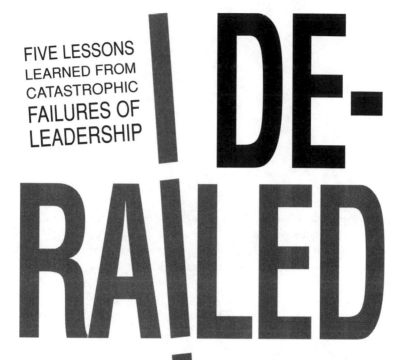

DE-
RAILED

TIM IRWIN, PH.D

THOMAS NELSON
Since 1798

NASHVILLE   DALLAS   MEXICO CITY   RIO DE JANEIRO   BEIJING

Published in Nashville, Tennessee by Thomas Nelson. Thomas Nelson is a trademark of Thomas Nelson, Inc.

Published in association with the literary agency of Wolgemuth & Associates, Inc.

Thomas Nelson, Inc., titles may be purchased in bulk for educational, business, fund-raising, or sales promotional use. For information, please e-mail SpecialMarkets@ThomasNelson.com.

Library of Congress Cataloging-in-Publication Data

Irwin, Tim, 1949-
    Derailed : five lessons learned from catastrophic failures of leadership / by Tim Irwin.
        p. cm.
    Includes bibliographical references and index.
    ISBN 978-1-59555-274-7
    1. Leadership. 2. Executive ability. I. Title.
    HD57.7.I79 2009
    658.4'092—dc22

                                                                    2009032905

Printed in the United States of America

09 10 11 12 WC   3 4 5 6

To James Daniel Irwin, Sr.
1922–2007
A man of quiet courage

CONTENTS

CONTENTS

ON TRACK FOR THE LONG HAUL

FOREWORD

In my work as a consultant, I can honestly say I've never discovered a company I thought was just too dumb to succeed. Nor have I yet found a CEO whom I felt could have been great if only he or she was smarter.

Now that may seem hard to believe, but I've come to the conclusion that in this era of nanosecond technology change and ubiquitous information, it is more difficult than ever to achieve and sustain a competitive advantage that is based on knowledge. Or put another way, it is relatively easy to accumulate the information and intellectual capital that is required to run a business successfully. As important as strategy, technology, and finance may be, there are few secrets left to be had.

And yet, as a society, we remain obsessed with the intellectual sciences and the impact they have on the success of people and the organizations they lead. Why? Because they are easier to measure and write articles about than less tangible areas that are more deserving of our focus.

What are the areas that deserve our focus? Well, when it comes to organizations, it's all about health. Is there a real culture? Is the executive team cohesive? Do employees know what makes the organization unique and what is required for success? Are there basic structures and systems in place to support all this?

And when it comes to the people who are responsible for

making those organizations healthy, it's all about character. Yes, character.

Now I realize that this word has been overused and misused, and much of its impact has been lost. But that's no reason to abandon it and go back to IQ tests and business school diplomas and résumés as our best predictors of success. Again, those are easier to measure and compare. But give me a leader with humility and integrity who graduated from Chico State University or SUNY at Buffalo or Colorado State University over a brilliant but character-challenged honor student from an Ivy League school any day.

The question for those who buy into this, of course, is how to go about defining, assessing, and developing character in a leader. There are just too many disparate definitions and theories out there.

Tim Irwin has tackled this challenge first by examining leaders who struggled, then dissecting their situations in search of common denominators. That's seems like a good idea to me, because we often learn and remember more about failures, our own and others', than we do from success.

But be warned that this book is not really about six famous leaders who derailed. It is about you. And me. And anyone who ever decided to accept a position of leadership. No one is immune from derailment. In fact, we're all just a moment away from doing something that could wound our organizations, our relationships, and our reputations—and perhaps earn us a chapter in a book about the struggles of leadership.

PATRICK LENCIONI
President, The Table Group
Author, *The Five Dysfunctions of a Team*
and several other national best sellers

PREFACE

The first time I met Bob Nardelli, I immediately liked him. He served with two other CEOs on a panel in a leadership forum that I moderated. He was smart, witty, challenging, and an excellent communicator. I have good friends who know all six of the individuals profiled in the upcoming chapters of this book, and there should be no doubt that these executives are bright, highly competent, resilient leaders. The boards that hired them had every reason to believe that these gifted individuals would provide outstanding leadership to their respective organizations. In each case, the board hired the leader because they believed the strengths of the new CEO were a good fit with the unique needs of the corporation at that time. Home Depot, for example, matured as an organization to the point where it needed a more disciplined management approach, and the board believed Nardelli's skills were exactly what were needed.

Each company's relationship with their newly hired CEOs began with great optimism. The expectation was that these individuals would serve for lengthy tenures and, at some point, after years of prosperity and success, execute a thoughtful succession of leadership. But somewhere along the line for each of the leaders profiled in this book, the board of directors concluded that the individual they collectively elected to lead their organization experienced a catastrophic failure of leadership.

The sources of information for the leader profiles were respected media, such as the *Wall Street Journal* and *Business Week*. My intent was to pull together information from an array of credible sources and to identify the reasons these individuals were eventually dismissed from their jobs. In fairness, there are at least two sides to every story. I have tried to provide a fair representation of what other reliable sources have said. This was not investigative journalism, but rather a summation of available public information used to create six illustrative case studies.

I have great appreciation for each of the six leaders profiled, for their tremendous competence and for what they have accomplished; very few people could do what they do. I have no doubt that each of these talented individuals will be successful, particularly when their strengths are a good match with the demands of a future endeavor. My respect for these six individuals made the leader profiles the hardest chapters in this book to write, because the focus became how each leader failed, even though each had a brilliant history of success in prior roles.

I chose to write about these particular leaders because they offered highly visible and compelling illustrations of individuals who derailed for the very reasons we can derail—a failure of character. I don't mean failed character in the sense of dishonesty that results in fraudulent behavior, but rather compromised character in a broader sense—for example, hubris or being dismissive of others.

At the outset, I feel it imperative to make clear that *Derailed* is ultimately not about the six profiled leaders . . . *it is about us!* The opening chapter is particularly important because it defines what derailment is and demonstrates why it is relevant to us, regardless of our present position or future aspirations. This book has two primary objectives: first, to help us understand how derailment occurs—the real point of the six leader profiles; second, to help us avoid a cataclysmic train wreck in our own careers—the subject of the second half of the book.

My hope is that you will find *Derailed* tremendously helpful. When we apply the principles in the upcoming pages, we will stay on track!

RUNNING OFF
THE RAILS

DE-
RAILED

DERAILED

"You're toast."

—TED TURNER

Aclient company known as one of the oldest, largest, and most successful enterprises in the electronics industry requested I attend a private dinner meeting that included the CEO, the COO, and the CFO. The rich mahogany wainscoting, heavy-beamed ceiling, lavish art, and opulent window treatments all contributed to the power atmosphere of an elite men's club near their global headquarters on the West Coast. The staff of attentive but professionally discreet waiters responded to our every whim, including a lavish array of expensive cabernets that flowed freely that night. As wine began to influence more of the conversation, the CEO and COO leaned toward each other and enjoyed a private laugh. A moment later the COO turned to me and asked if I knew a particular senior manager, a stunningly beautiful woman who ran the company's operation on another continent. With a sly grin, he said, "Now you know why Pete has that division report directly to him and why he goes over there so much!" A year later the board fired the CEO after quietly settling several sexual harassment suits.

Why would a powerful, influential, and wealthy man like

Pete so blatantly take advantage of his position? The very act of building an organization from insignificance to prominence, as Pete had done, potentially tempts hubris. Some leaders develop an entitlement mentality—"I made this company what it is, and I deserve to be treated with special deference"—when their company achieves great success, especially if the organization grew significantly during their tenure at the top, while others show the humility that often characterizes highly effective leaders.

Most companies place tremendous demands on top management. Fundamentally, a CEO must achieve financial results—that's why boards hire them—and the pressure to perform can be overwhelming. When I served in senior management of a public company, we knew that if we missed analysts' quarterly earnings projections by even a tiny amount, the market would punish us disproportionately. During one particularly challenging quarter, my company fell short of expectations by one cent per share, and our stock price dropped 20 percent the next day. A lot of individuals and institutional investors lost money. Those ultimately responsible for such results must be smart, tough-minded, resilient under stress, and able to handle the demands and complexity of leading a significant company.

When a company prospers, it's easy to see how the leader could naturally attribute the organization's success (deserved or not) to their own brilliance. I once attended a presentation during which a CEO pitched his company's services to one of the largest automotive parts manufacturers in the world. After the presentation, he boasted how he had done "a phenomenal job" of selling the merits of his company. I'm not making this up—when the elevator reached the ground level and we exited the building, he started jumping up and down, jubilantly singing, "I am the man . . . I am the man!"

Some leaders blinded by their own success even begin to treat the company like their personal ATM. Tyco's Dennis Kowalski bought a six-thousand-dollar shower curtain for his Manhattan apartment with company money. Merrill Lynch's John Thain spent over a million dollars redecorating his private office during a period in which the company's stockholders lost billions. His fourteen-hundred-dollar parchment trash can seemed like the perfect symbol of waste and excess.

We all possess a dark curiosity about the misfortunes of others. Would we rather watch a news program about ten trains arriving at the station on time or a story about a train that derailed, with vivid images of brave rescue workers removing bleeding survivors from the twisted wreckage? We will probably choose to watch the channel with breathless reporters in GORE-TEX rain suits tallying the latest count of fatalities. Pundit George Will commented, "Few things are as stimulating as other people's calamities observed from a safe distance."[1]

We have a special fascination when the mighty fall, such as the CEO of a famous company. Our more perverse side even likes it when someone receives his retribution and enters a court-house grimfaced, as we stay glued to cable TV, watching the perp walk of characters like Bernie Madoff. It's like watching a train wreck. We should look away, but we just can't.

DERAILMENT DEFINED

When a huge machine intended to pull great loads gets outside the crucial limits of two parallel steel rails, there are always certain and disastrous consequences. While train derailments occur for many reasons, including natural disasters or mechanical failure, the most memorable are those caused by human error. On September 12, 2008, an engineer of a California passenger train ignored a red warning light and a dispatcher's verbal warning before crashing into a parked freight train at forty miles per hour, resulting in 25 deaths and 135 injuries, 40 of them critical. Investigators discovered later that the engineer texted several teenagers just moments before the crash.[2]

The behavior of the person operating the train is the subject of *Derailed*. Any derailment causing the death or injury of innocents saddens us, but it seems particularly grievous when the derailment results from careless behavior of the engineer, who of all people should be responsible and worthy of our trust. An engineer texting someone when he should be paying attention to the warning systems is a gross violation of our trust.

All of us who work in organizations are the "engineers" of something, whether it is a team, a project, a department, or the mail room. While our derailment may not cause loss of life, it does negatively impact others and our own careers.

Derailment in our jobs means we are *off the rails*—we cannot proceed in our present jobs, just as a derailed train cannot continue on its intended path. Whether it's business, law, medicine, ministry, transportation, education, consulting, the military, skilled trades, art, music, or anything else, we work according to some set of expectations or requirements. If we work for an organization, typically there are requirements about how many hours a week we work or that we complete the tasks given us by someone in authority. Even the most unstructured occupations still have tracks on which they run. An entrepreneur has a boss—the customer. A failure to achieve the expected results in any work relationship can result in derailment.

CONSEQUENCES OF DERAILMENT

A person in a senior position, like the CEO, works for a governing authority, such as a board of directors, which can vote to remove the leader from his or her position. Though there may be many specific reasons for termination, they basically fall into three categories.

First, the company is not performing to expectations. The metrics by which a board makes that determination vary. The stock price may be languishing. The company's return on investment (ROI) may be poor, and it may be losing money.

The second category is more complex. The governing body concludes that even if the company is achieving its financial goals, the manager reaches them in a manner incongruent with the values and culture of the organization. Turnover in the senior ranks, poor morale, and general lack of endorsement by the members of the organization typify the symptoms of an organization with a leader not fulfilling a cultural mandate.

Category three, a combination of one and two, makes the decision to fire a leader easy. The leader failed to achieve results, *and* he or she violated the company's values or culture along the way.

Regardless of a board's stated reason for the dismissal of a leader, the chapters that follow examine the profiles of some well-known individuals to make the point that many derailments occur because epic weaknesses nullified a leader's towering strengths. Some recent cover photo CEO examples:

"Home Depot Board Ousts Chief"
— *The New York Times*, January 4, 2007

"Transition at Coca-Cola: Invester Paid a Price for Going It Alone"
—*Atlanta Journal & Constitution*, December 8, 1999

"Fiorina, High-Profile Female CEO, Fired as Head of Hewlett-Packard, Stock Up Sharply"
—Associated Press Newswires, February 9, 2005

"Starwood CEO Heyer to Leave—Board Sought Resignation after 2? Years at Helm"
— *The Wall Street Journal*, April 2, 2007

"Steve Case Quits as AOL Chairman Under Pressure—Time Warner Investors Blamed Him for Sell-Off in Stock After Big Merger"
— *The Wall Street Journal*, January 13, 2003

You are not asked to lead a substantive company without being smart, tough-minded, willful, skilled at political maneuvering, strategic . . . in short, a typical corporate leader; but a disabling weakness, a strength taken to excess, or a blind spot can derail even the most secure. Compelling examples of leaders who derailed abound, especially in the last few years.

During Bob Nardelli's six-year reign at Home Depot, the stock declined almost 8 percent—this concurrent with a period when the overall stock market was up almost 17 percent. "Nardelli displayed the skills of a seasoned operator, but garnered a hard-charging reputation for being tone deaf to the concerns of shareholders, employees and customers," asserted the *Atlanta Journal-Constitution*.[3] He became known for his arrogance, and he alienated the people he needed most. He seemed to eschew feedback so beneficial to any leader. He was "truth starved." Nardelli's military-style leadership produced some short-term profits but demoralized the Home Depot workforce. Customer satisfaction surveys took a nosedive.

Regardless of Nardelli's vision for the company, how could he ever achieve his objectives without the alignment, commitment, and loyalty of the Home Depot employees? He may have lacked self-awareness—a common denominator of those who derail. Paul J. Brouwer's 1964 *Harvard Business Review* classic, "The Power to See Ourselves," pointed to the foible decades ago.[4]

Durk Jager's brief and lackluster seventeen-month stint at the helm of consumer product giant Procter & Gamble demonstrates that it's about how we treat others—in this case, P&G's employees. *BusinessWeek* wrote that "Jager . . . ripped through P&G, bullying, gruffly talking to employees, and generating waves of initiatives. By publicly pitting himself against the corporate culture and the employees who lived it, Jager failed to gain a mandate, and his reorganization effort quickly failed."[5] Jager failed to create the support of those he needed most to implement his vision. How we treat members of our organization makes a huge difference in others' willingness to help us achieve the goals we most want to reach. Respect for others is foundational to the trust that leaders must create to be enthusiastically followed.

WHAT CAUSES DERAILMENT?

At a party a new acquaintance asked me about the subject of this book. I described how I was writing about famous corporate executives who derailed in their careers. When I mentioned that Carly Fiorina was on the list of ten or twelve individuals under consideration for the book, he said, "I used to work for her at Hewlett-Packard, and I don't think she was unsuccessful." In Fiorina's case, I agreed.

By any standard, Carly Fiorina was a rock star in the business world. *Fortune* magazine named her "The Most Powerful Woman in Business."[6] So how is it that Carly Fiorina qualified for the list?

Derailment and lack of success are different. Executives headed for derailment are often quite competent. They reach extraordinary heights in the corporate world through brilliance, hard work, strategic vision, and a track record of exceptional results. These individuals accomplish goals that exceed the capability of all but a talented few. To take the helm of an organization and routinely make decisions that impact many hundreds of thousands of shareholders, employees, customers, and vendors requires tremendous skill and confidence. The moxie to risk shareholders' money on a huge acquisition, such as when Fiorina merged with Compaq, exceeds the courage of most mortals.

But something happens. The expectation falls short, and

the plan to reach an intended destination goes awry or the expectation to fulfill perceived potential falls short. The assumed trajectory to move toward a high orbit more resembles one of those early rocket launches we see on the History Channel that start upward and quickly take a nosedive. Figure 1 illustrates the interruption of the expected potential of a promising career.

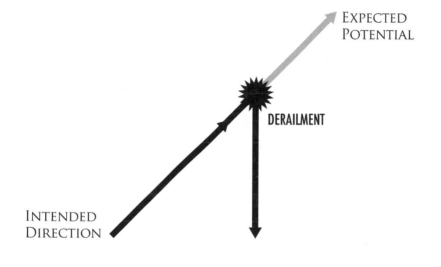

EXPECTED
POTENTIAL

DERAILMENT

INTENDED
DIRECTION

FIGURE 1

A governing board may fire a CEO for any number of reasons, but their required departure from the helm of the organization remains unarguable. Face-saving reasons for the leader's departure may be given (such as "Joe wants to spend more time with his family"), but in the inner sanctum of the boardroom where these decisions are made, the initiative of the governing body chooses to remove the person from their role.

Let me be clear that derailment resulting from fraudulent

behavior of a leader is *not* the subject of this book. Bernie Ebbers and Jeffrey Skilling committed fraud, which impacted the financial well-being of many thousands of employees and shareholders. They went to prison. While the leaders profiled in *Derailed* went off the tracks, fraud was *not* the reason.

What ultimately caused the derailment of the individuals profiled in upcoming chapters was a failure of character! The big lesson is that no matter how brilliant, charming, strategic, or commanding in presence a leader is, the consequences of a failed character are extraordinarily disabling and will bring down even the strongest among us. Similarly, if our character is inadequate, eventually we will miss the warning signals and slam into a parked freight train.

THE SHADOW LANDS

As part of an advanced scuba-diving certification, the requirement of a night dive loomed for me as the final and dreaded item on the checklist. Although I'm very comfortable in and around the water and a veteran of many daytime dives, night diving initially deprives us of an essential sense—sight. Our instructor insisted that night diving was a wonderful experience: "Seventy-five percent of sea life is nocturnal. Tonight, you'll barely believe your eyes."

At first I was like a skydiver frozen in the doorway of a jump plane, holding the rails and refusing to leap from the gently rocking boat. There had intentionally been no light for the last twenty minutes in the hope that our eyes could adjust to the moonless inky darkness. The tap on my shoulder signaled me to jump and gave no comfort to what seemed like a fool's errand in the making. "Remember, no flashlights until I give the okay!" our instructor repeated. The descent into oblivion was memorable!

Eventually we switched on our flashlights and the pageantry began. Bluish squid propelled themselves like ghosts across the expanse. Luminescent shrimp danced sideways on the ocean floor. Sea snakes weaved in and out of holes in the coral heads as if they were auditioning for Stephen King's latest novel.

To see clearly we must sometimes look into the darkness. To see what is really there, we must be willing to enter space, which appears devoid of the normal light on which we so heavily rely. The keenest insights into human behavior may emanate from our willingness to look not at what is light but what is dark . . . not from what is seen but what is unseen. Paradoxically, looking into darkness can be remarkably enlightening.

Our culture's obsession with perfection makes us reluctant to look at our own duality—that some of our impulses are noble, while others are not so benevolent . . . not that we've gone over to the dark side, but just that we *have* a dark side. Maybe we acknowledge our light and dark sides in a detached, abstract way, but to really open the door and look into the darkness isn't so easy. It's as though we have a quasi-dark side. Some might admit to having a "diet dark side"—just one calorie of dark side. Even in our most glaringly candid moments, we're reluctant to acknowledge that some of our inclinations are, at least, ineffective, if not dishonorable. Denial provides a safe way to sidestep our tension . . . or at least it seems that way.

To be more precise, the notion of a dark side needs a bit of calibration. Dr. Hannibal Lecter, the horrific antagonist in *The Silence of the Lambs*, defines the really dark side. Sister Teresa reflects the really light side. We probably dwell somewhere in between—the "shadow land." While many of our motives are altruistic and noble, others are less honorable.

When we live in the shadow lands of conflicted motives (as most of us do), we miss the clarity of the noonday sun and lose perspective about what's right. If and when we're willing to put some light on our own less-admirable qualities, it becomes painfully apparent that we all have *the latent potential to derail*, and many of our darker characteristics fully expressed can get us off track in a hurry. Shakespeare's *Macbeth* reveals that the dark side of some aspirations can compromise even the purest of souls. "Vaulting ambition, which o'erleaps itself/ And falls on th' other [side]."[7]

In moments of gut-wrenching candor, many self-aware leaders acknowledge a dark side to their character. Leaders who have great strengths also possess significant weaknesses, which cannot be ignored. Sadly, we, too, have the innate capacity for narcissism, arrogance, or disregard of other's opinions and interests in favor of our own. Perceptive executives control these impulses and choose to manage their darker sides' intrusion on decisions and relationships. Others—through blindness or foolish disregard—do not. Those who are more likely to stay out of trouble constantly remind themselves of their own vulnerability. Those most vulnerable live in denial. We should probably be honest about our duality, like the little girl with Santa in this cartoon.

"I'm like most people, I guess—a mixture of good and bad."

Some management experts emphasize the building and leveraging of our strengths in order to bring out the best in our capabilities at work. Peter Drucker wisely wrote, Build on your strengths to the point that your weaknesses become irrelevant.[8] While uplifting, such a perspective fails to fully address three realities. First, the unvarnished truth is that some weaknesses are so disabling, they can disqualify us—their impact is so significant that they exclude us from participation in leadership. We must address these besetting weaknesses.

Second, a given strength can quickly and easily become a weakness. Some attributes serve an individual well at a lower level of an organization, but then become weaknesses when his or her responsibility spans the enterprise's highest levels. Similarly, an overused strength can become a weakness.

Third, excessive stress compromises the performance of even the most resilient and sometimes drives us to give full expression to a flaw, which normally stays nice and tidy in the back rooms of our personalities.

SQUEEZING THE TUBE SHOWS YOU WHAT'S INSIDE

It cannot be overstated how much stress impacts our behavior. We can only look good for so long until stress strips away our façade and exposes our dark sides. It may take time or a significant amount of stress, but character weaknesses usually appear at some critical moment. It took eighteen years and 15,503 takeoffs and landings to expose a tiny nitrogen bubble in a titanium ingot used to manufacture the fan disk in a United Air jet flying from Denver to Chicago. When the exploding disk severed all the aircraft's hydraulics at thirty-seven thousand feet, what started as a routine flight became a terrorizing ordeal for passengers and crew.[9]

Insightful leaders monitor and manage their stress in order to mitigate its effect. Individuals who derail appear more susceptible to stress and its sinister tendency to fuel their dark sides. We all carry around some level of stress, but some high performers seem to be missing the protective emotional insulation that mitigates the deleterious effects of it. Their chronically high stress level fosters a greater susceptibility to the dark side of their character.

In recent years we've seen numerous character flaws surface in leaders whose narcissism and bad judgment resulted in stupendous suffering of stockholders, employees, and vendors, as well as the loss of people's trust in business in general. Stress is one of those pressures that squeeze out what's really inside us.

Given sufficient time and stress, those character-rooted derailment factors will surface. Many seasoned leaders report that recent economic conditions have created more stress than they've ever seen in their business careers!

LET'S TALK ABOUT YOU

Earlier I noted that derailment often results from a failure of character. Character forms our perspectives, guides our decisions, and influences how we treat others. Later in this book, when we unpack the character-rooted qualities that actually cause derailment, it will become apparent that there are only four. Though expressed in a variety of different behaviors, they are all tied to a lack of or failure of one of these four critical qualities:

1. Authenticity

2. Self-management

3. Humility

4. Courage

The unmitigated expression of the dark side of these four qualities renders a person in leadership or at any level of an organization ineffective, regardless of their other capabilities. The dark side of these four qualities is strikingly apparent in the lives of the six individuals who experienced catastrophic failures of leadership described in the forthcoming chapters.

Derailed focuses on what we can learn about how these compromising maladies can impact our leadership, how we treat others, and our capacity to make wise decisions. Behavior that decries wisdom, such as arrogance, power mongering, or the diminishment of others, can quickly derail any career. Failing to regulate our emotions, making decisions motivated by hubris, or treating others dismissively represents the menacing foibles to which we are susceptible.

The good news is that the light side of these same four qualities can be clearly tied to success in our work. To prevent our own derailment, it's critical to know what these qualities are and how we manifest their light side versus their dark side—which is the real aim of this book. The intended purpose of the profiles is not to disparage the leaders who derailed but to gain wisdom through their examples.

You may be thinking that while the misfortunes of famous leaders provide great entertainment, it's not that relevant to you; you are not a CEO and don't even have any aspirations to be a senior leader in your organization. Regardless of our positions in an organization or what stage or level our careers, derailment can happen to all of us. It's just not as newsworthy when it happens to someone other than the top dog. Most members of organizations who derail get off the tracks long before they reach the corner office on the top floor. We possess the very same potential to derail as the leaders to be profiled in the upcoming chapters (and for many of the same reasons).

A gifted young executive in his midthirties with an apparently bright future worked for a highly regarded national advertising firm. I observed him in a number of meetings and talked with coworkers who needed to collaborate with him on projects—it was like watching a train wreck in slow motion. He failed to keep his commitments to deliver certain work products to the team and arrived late or blew off meetings. His colleagues gradually closed him off from the team's projects, wouldn't include him in critical communication, and basically assigned him to the dustbin of irrelevance.

When his boss fired him, Fox Business News didn't scroll the announcement across the banner of that day's headlines, but this talented and promising young worker derailed nonetheless. The resulting consequence of derailment is that we're not allowed to continue our jobs. What gets us off track in our careers is not essentially different from what we see in high-profile leaders. Our derailment may result in fewer "deaths and injuries" and doesn't get plastered across the news, but the impact to us is the same. As the cartoon below points out, we'll be moving on.

"I believe, Merkin, that my action today frees you to unleash your God-given talents, and pursue your dreams, in some other venue."

WHAT MESSAGES COULD
YOU BE IGNORING?

Just as the California engineer received (and ignored) the warning signals about the parked freight train ahead, we, too, may be the recipients of early warning signals. While colorful, bold, and even entertaining in some instances, leaders who derail misread the symptoms of their own doom. They fail to take the corrective actions needed to sustain their viability as a leader. Particularly in the early stages, signals of derailment may not be a glaring red light alerting us of trouble ahead; the warning signs are likely to be more subtle. Over time the young advertising executive simply became marginalized; his termination occurred months after the more subtle signals indicated trouble ahead.

In corporate Japan, senior management sends a not-so-subtle message by assigning out-of-favor executives to the "window seat" or "window job" (*mado giwa zoku*).[10] The new assignment requires the banished executive to sit by a window with nothing to do. Before shriveling into total irrelevance, the holder of the window job no doubt morosely ponders what could have been of their life and career. One of my U.S. clients refers to some poor performers as "Gentlemen Cs." This disparaging term marginalizes the person as "nice" but wholly ineffective in their job. In tough economies, these "C performers" are often the first to go. Early warning signals are the topic of greater detail in a later chapter, but we should always pay attention to the following signs:

- Not getting a promotion

- Not getting assigned to a strategic project team

- Being relocated to the "cubicle of despair"
- Being left out of important meetings
- Not being in the loop on important communication
- Being banished to a lackluster team

Whether subtle or direct, no matter how it's communicated, we never want to hear the words media mogul Ted Turner used to tell his own son that he was about to be fired from his job as a promotions manager at Turner Home Entertainment—"You're toast!"[11]

PROFILES IN
DERAILMENT

DE-
RAILED

PROFILE # 1
BOB NARDELLI

"I've attended over a thousand shareholder meetings . . . and I am totally distressed to see the amount of arrogance I've seen today . . . You don't respond to anything. I mean, what are we paying you $245 million to do? . . . It doesn't matter how talented you are. If you don't listen to people, if you don't interact and you aren't humble and decent, you will destroy this company."

—SAMUEL YAKE
Home Depot shareholder,
at the 2006 shareholder meeting

At five foot ten and 195 pounds, Robert "Bob" Nardelli's dream of playing professional football was a stretch. "The rest of the world got bigger," he recalled, "and I didn't grow any-more."[1] Perhaps this was when the chip began to form on Nardelli's shoulder. From that point on, he seemed wrought with something to prove, if not to the NFL, then to the hard-hitting, high-dollar corporate world.

He earned a business degree and took a job at General Electric where his father had worked a lifetime in the factories. On GE soil, Nardelli quickly became a go-to guy. Though never a blazing intellect, he worked the longest hours, tackled the toughest turnarounds, and became, in the words of GE's CEO at the time, Jack Welch, "the best operating executive I've ever seen."[2] He was duly nicknamed "Little Jack."

He was primed to succeed his namesake as GE's next CEO, but he came up short yet again, and this time it had nothing to do with his height. Welch informed Nardelli in November 2000 that the polished Ivy Leaguer Jeff Immelt would be Welch's replacement.[3] Stunned and furious, Nardelli retorted, "You've got to tell me why. Tell me what I could have done better. Tell me the numbers weren't there, the innovation, the talent, development, the relationship with the Street; give me a reason."[4] "I had to go with my gut," Welch told him.[5] Although Welch handled it in a respectable manner, discerning onlookers were still left wondering the real reason behind his gut feeling about Nardelli.

The huge disappointment was a perfect opportunity for Nardelli to take a hard look at himself and evaluate who he was as an employee and a leader, to determine why and how he was not the man for the top job at GE—and would never have been, according to Welch.[6] The reasons for falling short were not as tangible as physical stature. They were internal flaws, character flaws that were difficult to see but not impossible to remedy.

Unfortunately, the assessment opportunity was short-lived (and, given his track record, would have been disregarded anyway). About ten minutes after Welch let him go, Nardelli was offered the CEO position at Home Depot from Ken Langone, who was then on the boards of both GE and Home Depot.[7] Nardelli's charge: tidy the chaos of Home Depot's rapid, uncontrolled expansion.

Nardelli was bound to catch the big break. His tenacity and

obsessive efficiency made him a productivity god in a world of systems and structure. The problem was that these same qualities hid dark sides that would ultimately derail him. That they existed before his time at Home Depot is probable if not provable—they were at least a major reason he was passed over at GE—however, one thing is certain. Under the big lights of the world's second-largest retailer, no faults remain hidden for long.

A DIFFERENT KIND OF GROWTH

Founders Arthur Blank and Bernie Marcus had grown Home Depot at a scorching pace since 1978. It had become a decentralized, entrepreneurial, $46 billion company—"a haven for independent-minded employees . . . who got things done but didn't always play by the traditional corporate rules."[8]

"Blank and Marcus had a simple business strategy: continuous expansion. In 24 years they had grown Home Depot from a single warehouse store to a 1,155-store giant." Yet by the turn of the century, all that unbridled entrepreneurial spirit was feeling some backlash. "Costs were out of control, same-store (stores open for at least a year) sales were flat, profit growth had slowed, and the share price had dropped." To make matters worse, "Lowe's, Home Depot's primary competitor, was doing far better."[9]

The founders' vision and energy had inspired an innovative, high-retention culture. Yet, despite their orange-blooded passion, by 2000, Blank and Marcus began to see their most significant oversight: they never prepared leaders inside the company to replace them.

"Because Arthur and I were always there," Marcus admitted,

"our people never developed the talent they need to run the company. Our presence created this wall."[10]

The two leaders had already been quietly searching for their replacement when Nardelli became available, so they wasted no time scooping him up.[11] The news came as a shock to Home Depot employees. "If any of us had vaguely considered that one day there'd be a new CEO, we would have expected an internal hire," said Tom Taylor, eastern division president.[12]

Though the outcome remained to be seen, the hiring of an outsider was perhaps a bigger mistake than not training an inside leader in the first place. While the company's entrepreneurial clutter was certainly in need of straightening, one can only wonder if the subsequent six years of trouble might have been avoided without such a hasty, counterintuitive hire. One mistake had been made in lack of successor planning. The second could have been avoided.

To say Home Depot was on the wrong track in 2000 would be inaccurate. More precisely, the company was in need of a thorough tune-up. It was a highly innovative but grossly inefficient company—like a first-class train that couldn't serve its meals on time.

Nardelli came in wearing three decades of something-to-prove on his shoulder, and his something involved more than tidiness and timeliness. It would entail a complete overhaul of the very engine that drove Home Depot to success—its entrepreneurial spirit.

Businessweek columnist Bruce Nussbaum summed the ensuing Nardelli era well. "Nardelli," he wrote, "came into Home Depot with a managerial style that was already obsolete and being replaced at GE by Immelt with his emphasis on eco-imagination. Autocratic top-down, command and control works great when you focus on process—cost and quality. Six Sigma measures all that stuff wonderfully. Nardelli couldn't see beyond this . . . He shifted Home Depot . . . to a new contracting business that could more easily be controlled and measured."[13]

Nardelli immediately hired human resources (HR) chief Dennis Donovan (formerly of GE) to help centralize human capital management and minimize store autonomy. This may well have been his first mistake. He also instituted Six Sigma practices—the quality-control process originally introduced by Bill Smith at Motorola that seeks to measure and manage the highest levels of corporate efficiency—to generate metrics and gauge effectiveness of all divisions and processes. Metrics were not foreign to the Home Depot executives, but the degree of control Nardelli's wielded was at the far end of the leadership spectrum.

Nardelli strongly believed that better processes led to better quality and higher profits. "He increased information technology spending by 20 percent. In 2003 alone, he spent $400 million on inventory shipping and tracking systems. He substituted 157 different employee evaluation forms with two and required salaried personnel from the CEO down to be rated by co-workers, above and beneath them, and salaries to be based on the scores."[14] All told, "he invested more than $1 billion in new technology, such as self-checkout aisles and inventory management systems that generated reams of data. He declared that he wanted to measure virtually everything that happened at the company and hold executives strictly accountable for meeting their numbers."[15]

With military precision, Nardelli attacked and destroyed

what he perceived were enemies to greater productivity. In doing so, he was only creating more. In 2001, the analyst Donald Trott told Jennifer Pellet of *Chief Executive*: "With Bernie and Arthur, the approach culturally was, 'We're part of the troops like you guys and we're going into battle with you.' But Nardelli does not look comfortable in that orange apron. His body language is more 'I am the general up on the hill with the binoculars; you guys go take on the enemy.'"[16]

TAKING THE "HOME" OUT OF HOME DEPOT

As processes tightened, the individual liberties employees had always known diminished. Calling executives in for weekend meetings, Nardelli frequently reminded them their responsibilities were not a job but a life. Blank and Marcus had motivated employees with hugs and cheers. Nardelli was a sharp contrast. He seemed bent on motivating people by fear and control. This he denied, claiming the only reason one should be fearful is for lack of commitment. Yet, his dogged insistence on perfection and adherence to protocol told a different story.[17]

Nardelli seemed far more concerned about his processes than his people. He was indifferent about developing relationships with employees, at times taking actions that would suggest he was adamantly against it. "He frequently inflamed managers by sending insensitive e-mail messages about cluttered aisles and poorly lighted displays."[18] Former employees claimed he was a closed, inflexible, and demanding micromanager who treated people like cogs in his well-oiled machine.

Case in point was the private elevator to his twenty-second-floor office in Vinings, Georgia. His exclusive use of it eliminated any chance he'd share an elevator ride with an employee. The computer terminal on his desk allowed him to watch every aisle, parking lot, checkout station, and shopping cart in any of the 1,962 stores.[19]

If he actually trusted employees, the sentiment didn't transfer outside Nardelli's own head. People worked in constant twofold fear: of failure and of job loss. In an article in *Business Week* written after his firing, one former executive confessed: "Every single week you shuddered when you looked at email because another officer was gone."[20]

Nardelli shoved the interpersonal relationship standard to the concrete floor when his initial cost-cutting measures included slashing full-time jobs, capping wages, and recruiting former military officers to run the stores. It didn't take long before staff morale and customer service began to collapse under Nardelli's autocratic regime. The number of part-time employees skyrocketed from 26 percent to as high as 50 percent in 2002 as "he gutted the retail side by cutting the smiling, knowledgeable salespeople who were so helpful to customers."[21]

It should come as no surprise that one of Nardelli's favorite sayings was, "Facts are friendly." He seemed unconcerned that the same be true of people—especially himself.[22]

"One recurring criticism of Nardelli," reported an article in the *Atlanta Journal Constitution*, "was that the General Electric veteran went overboard in applying GE's industrial-strength operating techniques at a company that was bred on the motto: 'Make love to the customer.' Store staffers frequently complained that they spent more time on paperwork and procedures than they did helping customers . . . one longtime

Georgia manager lamented, 'The customer is caught up in the seventh dimension of Six Sigma.'[23]

Slowly but surely, the once happy-go-lucky Home Depot became a mathematical equation. As the earnings went up under the Nardelli equation—they had nearly doubled by the time of his departure—the stock went down (at a time when Lowe's soared 200 percent) and the human spirit went out. The company's trip along this track could only last so long.

HIS WAY WAS THE HIGHWAY

Barry Henderson, an equities analyst at T. Rowe Price, held a common conclusion about Nardelli's derailment. He believes alienating employees and angering stockholders were Bob Nardelli's two primary mistakes at Home Depot.[24] While he may be accurate, I believe there is a lot more to it.

The sum total of Nardelli's leadership at Home Depot was a dramatic shift in the spirit of the company and subsequently the service of their ever-satisfied customers. The 98 percent turnover in the company's top executives—with 56 percent of the new hires coming in from outside the company—supports this notion. People simply couldn't and wouldn't work passionately for their command-and-control leader. In this respect, Nardelli was no leader at all. He was a dictator who demanded compliance.

If there is a generalization about Nardelli's mistake, it is that he usurped Home Depot's identity. This was the result of a much deeper mistake than alienating employees and angering stockholders.

Nardelli displayed an unprecedented level of arrogance at

Home Depot. It was his way or the highway. His tone-deaf response to criticism was only slightly overshadowed by an ego that served as the antithesis of his physical stature. His intolerance for imperfect people and those who could not be controlled sent only one message: get it right or get out.

High expectations are not uncommon in the corporate world, but Nardelli's gross level of inflexibility is. Not only did it handcuff employees, but it removed from the grid the daily seizing of spontaneous opportunities that had grown Home Depot in the first place. Certainly, employees ought to be held accountable—especially executives—but not to the degree that they display a crippling fear of not only the failure but the leader to whom they are obligated to follow. The circumstances exemplifying Home Depot's culture during Nardelli's reign point out what I view to be his real mistakes: unbearable arrogance, lack of courage in leadership, and an intense distrust of others.

Nardelli truly believed his presence and processes could take the orange giant where it needed to go. Yet, as the engine wheels began to wobble, we were reminded once again that no leader is that good—especially one convinced that he is.

The pivotal turning point in Bob Nardelli's reign as Home Depot chairman and CEO came at the 2006 annual Home Depot shareholder's meeting. "Smarting from investor and consumer criticism that he was again failing and now overpaid, Nardelli insulated himself. . . . [He] asked his board not to come and refused to answer shareholder questions. . . . Rather than listen and change failing practices, Nardelli dropped the unfavorable metrics that highlighted failure, i.e. 'moving the goal posts.'"[25]

Management professor Michael Useem, director of Wharton's

Center for Leadership and Change Management, wrote that Nardelli's actions "will forever serve as a symbol of the tone deaf chief executive."[26]

Nardelli's failures came to a tangible head at the conclusion of the 2006 meeting. Samuel Yake, a shareholder in attendance, echoed the sentiment of not only most in the room that day but also the vast majority of the current and former Home Depot employees.

"Mr. Chairman," began Yake, "I want to just make one point . . . Arrogance is a great destroyer in corporate America and really human relations. Arrogance is a terrible poison . . . I came today wanting to buy more stock. I love Home Depot. I shop there. I've read *Built to Last*, a great book. I love your founders . . . It's a wonderful company. And I don't understand it. I'm really perplexed. I'm not an opponent of the company . . . Why not take questions? . . . If you don't listen to people, if you don't interact, and you aren't humble and decent you will destroy this company. And that's my only point."

"Thank you," Nardelli replied. "Thank you, Samuel." He then adjourned the meeting.[27]

A few weeks later Nardelli was out as chairman and CEO. The widespread reaction told the tale of an arrogant leader who never quite learned from his shortcomings, and who couldn't have left soon enough.

"It's amazing, the reaction of people on my floor. People are openly ecstatic. High-fiving," said an Atlanta store operations manager only hours after the January 3 announcement. "There's a group talking about going to happy hour at noon."[28]

At that time, one was only left to hope Nardelli's next tenure would end with a different sort of celebration. Such hopes were dashed when in April 2009 he was ousted again, this time from Chrysler after only twenty-one months.

Of Nardelli's second exit in the same decade, the *Wall Street Journal*'s Heidi Moore wrote, "Demanding shareholders may not have been a problem at Chrysler, but its financial backer, Cerberus, is being slowly squeezed out by the government. Nardelli wasn't as beloved by his new government overlords. In a Senate hearing in December, Nardelli was openly disdained by Sen. Bob Corker of Tennessee, who compared Chrysler to a gold-digger that is 'just dating until you can get married to get enough money to survive.'"[29]

While no one will argue that Nardelli is highly capable, he will likely not fulfill his potential as a leader until he learns what all great leaders know: greatness does not result from *competence* only; it flows from an inspired workforce who trusts the *character* of its leader.

PROFILE # 2
CARLY FIORINA

"In a revealing moment in 2001, Fiorina returned to the Stanford campus to deliver the commencement speech . . . for all the bravery evident in both her life and that speech, Fiorina came across as astonishingly caught up in her own story.

In the half-hour talk, she used the word 'I' 129 times."
—GEORGE ANDERS
author of *Perfect Enough*

In the late 1990s, Hewlett-Packard faced a defining moment in its history. Caught in its longest financial slump, the H-P Way was under fire. As the turn of the century approached, the company of inventors was in need of reinventing. It appeared the father of Silicon Valley success had grown old and could no longer keep stride with the young bucks of the computing industry. H-P's revenues from continuing operations had grown by just 7 percent in fiscal 1999. Compared to Sun Microsystems' swift 20 percent growth during the same period, H-P was being lapped. Even PC giant IBM managed to grow its revenues by more than 12 percent that year.

H-P's earnings growth had also been mediocre. A December 1999 article in the *Financial Times* reported that over the previous five years, its earnings had only grown at an average rate of 15.1 percent, against an industry average of 25.6 percent. As a result, Wall Street analysts were predicting a decline in H-P's earnings in the first half of fiscal 2000.[1]

As a solution, the company planned to spin off Agilent, its technical equipment division and one of three core business lines. H-P needed the transition to be managed well. But the company's vaunted light-reigned, entrepreneurial culture was diluting sales and product marketing efforts, making it clear that H-P needed tighter organizational focus. It needed to clarify its brand and sync it with a new operational model that could pace with a new generation and new set of competitors—especially the likes of newbie Dell Computer Corp., which was gaining ground quickly.

For the first time since its beginnings in a Palo Alto garage in 1938, Hewlett-Packard stepped outside its walls to usher in a leader they believed could solve their problems and re-stake their claim as "the legendary corporation that helped spawn Silicon Valley."[2]

"To jumpstart the moribund company," explained a February 17, 2003, *BusinessWeek* article, "the board brought in . . . the charismatic Carlton S. Fiorina. Shake things up she did."[3] It is an accurate assessment. But perhaps the connotation is more diplomatic than it should be.

"Chainsaw Carly," as she would become known, had successfully led the spin-off of Lucent from AT&T in 1996. Moreover, she had transformed Lucent, once a "humdrum maker of phone-equipment, into an Internet player" by rolling out a $90 million brand-building campaign and fast-tracking product development from Bell-labs engineers.[4] In 1998, she was made president of Lucent's $19 billion global service-provider business.[5] It capped a strong track record that gave no indication of ceasing.

Fast Company mainstay George Anders reported that H-P's CEO headhunter, Jeff Christian, was "struck" by Fiorina's problem-solving prowess. "At every juncture except one (a Lucent-Philips joint venture to make telephone handsets), she had been able to fix things. She had a methodology. She would go into an area and spend a lot of time listening at first. She was a big believer that organizations already contained a lot of the right ideas," explained Christian.[6]

On July 17, 1999, with great expectations, Carly Fiorina was officially named H-P's chief executive. The *Wall Street Journal* reported she was "the first woman to head one of the nation's 20-biggest public firms. The appointment shows that H-P is serious about continuing to revamp its stodgy image."[7]

Fiorina seemed poised to turn things around as she was unreserved in fingering H-P's problems and prophesying their solutions.

Financial Times writer Louise Kehoe noted that, according to Fiorina, H-P's sales performance had been hampered by a lack of collaboration and passive, fragmented marketing. "Ms. Fiorina," wrote Kehoe, "makes no secret of H-P's problems, most of which, she implies, are of its own making."[8] She notes that Fiorina felt the company's founders, Bill Hewlett and David Packard, "feared the downside of big." They created a company culture that ensured independence and agility but simultaneously welcomed inefficiency, a lack of cohesion, and diluted marketing. Fiorina liked to cite the 750 internal employee training Web sites as her case in point. "We have," said Fiorina, "a lot of soloists in this company and what we need is an orchestra."[9]

Fiorina got right to tidying what she considered to be an unkempt giant by launching an integrated, global advertising campaign before her tenure was six months old. With an implication that the strategy would maintain the strengths of the H-P brand, the tangible reality was quite different. Fiorina methodically began to strip the company of its inconspicuous identity and dress it with a flashy designer look that fit her well.

A NEW BUT UNBEFITTING LOOK

Before joining H-P, Fiorina had already gained a reputation for her hard-charging, high-fashion style. She fit well in sales and marketing circles where self-promotion was acceptable and the limelight was your best friend. She felt H-P should join that circle. "In certain respects, Fiorina did exactly what she had been asked to do," explained a 2005 *Time* magazine article. "Hewlett-Packard . . . was a pocket-protector paradise, its culture defined by the H-P way: paternal, collaborative, entre-preneurial, community minded and inconspicuous. . . . Fiorina was brought in to drive a stake through that squishy culture's heart. . . . The company needed to reposition itself in a new, net-worked environment. Fiorina . . . was well versed in the dangers of cultural inertia."[10]

It took little time for Fiorina's cultural makeover of H-P to take hold . . . and begin turning sour. While no one was arguing the need for a more unified front, H-P insiders began to sense that Fiorina's change strategy was less about H-P and more about promoting its new boss.

In attempts to confront the problems that ailed H-P, Fiorina shaved the number of H-P's business units from eighty-three to only a handful and consolidated executive authority through her office. She then stemmed financial losses in the PC division through extensive layoffs.[11] Although the measures allowed the company to cut costs, they were in stark contrast to the long-admired, fraternal culture of the company, and offended disciples of the H-P Way.

Fiorina's make-or-break moment occurred in 2002, when she pushed through a controversial merger with Compaq, overcoming opposition from board member and Hewlett family member Walter Hewlett in the most expensive proxy battle ever fought. Although the merger made H-P the immediate market leader in personal computers, Fiorina's treatment of Walter Hewlett showed a gross disregard for H-P's roots, something her critics had been charging almost from the beginning.

Had the merger proved to catapult the company into the limelight as Fiorina expected, it is reasonable to think she might still hold her position. As it happened, however, the $19 billion acquisition and merger with Compaq fell well short of profit targets. Not only did this bring into question Fiorina's leadership, it brought out another side of the boss that few had yet to see.

"In 2003," explained the *Time* article, "despite Fiorina's promises that operating margins would reach 3%, the company's PC division earned a meager 0.1% on $21.2 billion in sales. And last August, the company's Enterprise Servers and Storage Group, which sells to corporate customers, reported a $208 million loss for the quarter. As a furious Fiorina reacted by publicly firing the server unit's boss and two others, the board began to take a harder look at her performance."[12]

As the H-P insiders and the broader business community became more confident the Compaq merger was a bust, Fiorina became more defensive about her ability to execute the company's strategy. She turned, instead, to blaming others for the company's failure to meet earnings expectations. The board then began suggesting she spread the leadership load, perhaps to a new chief of operation. She strongly resisted the notion. While many had their hunches, the makeover had not been so clearly personal to Fiorina until then.

"The tide really began turning against Fiorina," *Business Week* writer Ben Elgin wrote, "following H-P's massive profit shortfall in the third quarter of [2004] . . . H-P's second miss in five quarters. . . . Although Fiorina fired three top sales executives for the miss, the board's doubts about its CEO grew. At the same time, the board's prodding of Fiorina to bolster H-P's operations talent went largely unheeded."[13]

As Fiorina held firm, H-P's stock price continued to fall— at one point to 55 percent below its pre-Carly price. The board tightened its position and eventually made it clear to Fiorina that they planned to shift some of her operational responsibilities to her direct reports, potentially chief strategy and technology officer Shane Robison. According to sources close to the discussions, it was their intention not to fire Fiorina in this process but rather to help her succeed. "The board felt," wrote Pui-Wing Tam in the *Wall Street Journal,* "Ms. Fiorina had great abilities."[14]

Fiorina strongly resisted this plan, citing two primary reasons: 1) Robison's lack of experience in running a company, and 2) it was the CEO's prerogative to delegate operations, not the board's. Because of her resistance, the board asked for her resignation, on the grounds that they needed a leader with more operational talent.

"As a light rain drizzled outside," explained *Business Week*'s Ben Elgin, "the directors stewed over their star CEO's failure to execute her ambitious plan for the company. In addition, directors were concerned about the 'board's inability to work constructively with [Fiorina],' according to an H-P insider. The next day, they asked Fiorina to step down. And on Wednesday, Feb. 9, at 5 a.m. Pacific time, H-P stunned the world, announcing Fiorina's dismissal, ending her five-and-a-half year stint atop one of the legends of Silicon Valley."[15] The board finally concluded, explained a *Time* article, "that Fiorina had one significant weakness as a chief executive: she just wasn't very good at running the business."[16]

On the day the ouster was announced, some employees raised their glasses and H-P's stock price jumped as much as 10.5 percent at one point, settling up 6.9 percent. "The stock is up . . . on the fact that nobody liked Carly's leadership all that much," said Robert Cihra, an analyst with Fulcrum Global Partners. "The Street had lost all faith in her and the market's hope is that anyone will be better."[17]

WHY FIORINA EVENTUALLY FACED DEMISE

Fiorina's rock-star image and tendency toward self-promotion exacerbated the tensions brought on by her operational changes. Morale dropped as did the very identity that had made H-P a computing icon. "She had a flair," described Tam in the *Wall Street Journal,* "for marketing and public speaking, and jetted world-wide to visit customers, employees, shareholders and world leaders. She greatly expanded H-P's fleet of corporate jets and attracted criticism for everything from her hairstyle to her designer suits."[18]

In the end, her high-profile style, penchant for travel in Gulfstream jets, and abrupt management methods were deeply at odds with the paternal, understated culture of H-P. She was a self-assured, extroverted salesperson in a company full of quiet, introverted engineers. If anything, she needed to lean to their side of the spectrum, not the other way around. Nearing the end of Fiorina's tenure, Richard Hagberg, a consultant from San Mateo, California, told her that "rock stars were probably not going to be accepted by . . . a bunch of engineers." But instead of reaching out, Fiorina isolated herself. Unlike the leaders before her, she rarely socialized with H-P staffers.[19]

"Ms. Fiorina's leadership was also marked by a drop in morale," wrote *Wall Street Journal*'s Pui-Wing Tam. "She had . . . many fans in the business world. Yet inside H-P, she was a highly polarizing figure who stirred deep animosity from many veteran employees."[20]

To the board and many on the outside, Fiorina symbolized the very image the company needed to prop them back on track. But in this case, opposites did not attract. Over time, the perception of Fiorina as a self-promoting, stubborn aristocrat could not be the face of such a collegial company.

FAILING TO FACE THE FACTS

Though Fiorina was hired explicitly to take on certain operational problems caused by the longstanding culture of the company, she made the fatal mistake of appearing to dismiss it entirely. Even if one assumes her intentions were for the company's good, Fiorina's flippant attitude toward its culture was made most evident by the manner in which she conducted the 2002 Compaq proxy battle against director Walter Hewlett, son of the cofounder—what one Fiorina biographer called "an enormous public struggle for H-P's soul."[21] Because of the manner in which she conducted that disagreement, Fiorina came to personify, especially in the minds of employees, the forces that were destroying all that was good about H-P.

"Based on the belief that smart people will make the right choices if given the right tools and authority," Peter Burrows explained in *Business Week*, "'Bill and Dave' [H-P's founders] pushed strategy down to the managers most involved in each business. The approach worked. Not only did H-P dominate most of its markets, but low-level employees unearthed new opportunities for the company. 'H-P was always the exact opposite of a command-and-control environment,' says former CEO Platt."[22]

Prior to Fiorina's arrival, H-P fostered an environment where workers felt obligated to be involved and speak up when something needed fixing or could be improved. Carly changed that environment to one of distrust and fear. People no longer felt they could or should speak up. Nor did they feel they had any say in the direction the company was headed. It was a shift too far off track from which to recover.

For certain, many leaders make wrong moves that appear to position them at odds with the wishes of the people they lead. Such wrong moves are recoverable when the body of the leader's actions supports a different notion that is harmonious to the culture. This was not the case with Fiorina. Her actions—namely during and following the Compaq merger—created a head of steam in support for an image of her that was 180 degrees from the H-P Way. It was one thing to lead the Way in a new direction; it was another thing to turn her back on the Way altogether. The result, according to author Peter Burrows, was "a widespread sense of resignation." Burrows cited Jeffery Sonnenfeld, associate dean of the Yale School of Management, who asserted, "The proxy fight didn't enhance the company's reputation for integrity . . . To bludgeon a guy that represents at least 50 percent of the owners showed a tremendous lack of respect for corporate governance."[23]

When confronted with the facts, a wiser, humbler Fiorina might have confessed her shortcomings and won her critics over, knowing she could only take the company as far as it would allow her to take it. It is still surprising that chief executives still fall into the belief that they are bigger than the company they run. Instead, she displayed defensiveness and an inability to admit her failures, at one point asserting, "I'm running the business the way I think it ought to be run."[24] Said one former H-P executive, "We're all supposed to be in the same boat but she wasn't in that boat with us."[25]

In fact, Fiorina's finger-pointing while in office continued after her departure. In her 2006 memoir, *Tough Choices*, she skirted the two primary indictments against her—poor execution and a lack of a unified vision—instead of using the platform to exonerate herself. "Perhaps," she wrote, "I underestimated people's ability to step up to what had to be done. Nevertheless, it is also true that for many it was just easier to blame the new CEO and bestow a new nickname: Chainsaw Carly."[26]

As skilled as Fiorina was and still is, upon reflection it would seem that her tough choices at H-P were tougher than she realized then, or now. "To this day," she wrote, "I underestimate people's capacity to abuse my trust and the insecurity that sometimes drives them."[27] *Barron's* Ray Tiernan and Jay Palmer concluded: "When faced with tough choices, Carly Fiorina rarely made the wrong one, or so it would seem."[28] In fact, her dismissiveness of others couldn't have been a worse choice.

On Fiorina's downfall, it is perhaps simplest to conclude that what led to her derailment were the shortcomings she saw abundantly in others but did not acknowledge in herself. Fiorina was always quick to call others to the rug when they did not deliver but was dismissive when called to the rug herself. Failure was always someone else's fault—even her own failure. This trait, in combination with her penchant for promoting herself did nothing but culminate into a perception that she was both too self focused and disingenuous.

In hindsight, Fiorina was not a good fit with the H-P culture, and she bears significant responsibility for not "managing upward" well in dealing with H-P's board. It is highly probable that if the Compaq merger had been successful, Fiorina would still have her job, despite the numerous problems mentioned here. Most would argue that she is an extremely bright and highly capable individual.

Fiorina recently took steps which will lead to her candidacy for a United States Senate seat from California. While I am certainly not a political analyst, my sense is that the people of California would be well served to have such a competent individual in their service. Her role as a senator would likely play to her strengths. She is an excellent communicator and would bring profound insight to the significant challenges faced by the United States today. It will be great political theater to see if California voters will afford her the opportunity.

PROFILE #3
DURK JAGER

"He is a brutal man of limited tastes. Doing his job is what he likes best."

——FORMER PROCTER & GAMBLE INSIDER
describing former CEO Durk Jager[1]

When longtime Procter & Gamble (P&G) CEO Edwin Artzt retired in 1995, the company's board replaced him with the effective and likable consensus builder John Pepper, the fifty-six-year-old head of Procter & Gamble's international business. The board also created a post for Dutch-born Durk Jager, fifty-one-year-old head of Procter & Gamble's U.S. business. Tough, autocratic, and a former protégé of Artzt, Jager was named chief operating officer.[2]

P&G was suffering from slowing sales, a lack of revolutionary products, and stagnating earnings growth kept positive only by cost cutting, hardly a long-term strategy. "P&G was in danger," wrote *BusinessWeek*'s Robert Berner, "of becoming another Eastman Kodak Co. or Xerox Corp., a once-great company that had lost its way."[3] To solve its problems, the board believed the company needed to develop products and brands more quickly and launch them globally, rather than market-to-market as it had always done. It brainstormed a profound restructuring effort called "Organization 2005." The goal: double sales by the end of 2005 to approximately $70 billion.

The board also believed that P&G's culture needed examination. So established, bureaucratic, and uniform that outsiders called employees "proctoids," the company culture seemed to bear the blame for its lack of speed in generating ideas and rolling out new products. Known as uncompromising, passionate about speed, and an outstanding strategist, Chief Operating Officer Jager seemed to be perfectly suited to run day-to-day operations. In the words of CNN's Katrina Brooker, P&G needed a "serious kick in the pants,"[4] and Jager was wrought with the skills and personality to deliver it.

On January 1, 1999, John Pepper officially retired as chief executive, paving the way for the hard-charging Jager to become CEO. The board believed P&G needed a rebel, someone to shake things up. Pepper's generous endorsement of Jager swelled board and Wall Street confidence that the new leader could pull off the simultaneous organizational and cultural changes the $37 billion giant needed. "Durk Jager personifies the essential qualities that will be critical to realizing the goals and vision we are pursuing," said Pepper. "He is an outstanding strategic thinker and a passionate advocate for greater innovation and speed. He has led truly fundamental strategic changes, such as efficient consumer response and simplification and standardization, that have had an impact not only on P&G, but also have reshaped markets and changed the rules of the game."[5]

Although Pepper's optimism was well founded given Jager's rich history of organizational success, Jager's changes over the next seventeen months revealed another side of his character and leadership that no amount of optimism could undo.

THE PACE IS AS IMPORTANT AS THE CHANGE

No one debated that P&G could use some streamlining. While it boasted four times the sales of competitor Colgate-Palmolive and three times those of Kimberly-Clark, and while its three hundred–plus brands were available in 140 countries, the fact remains that P&G had stopped growing. P&G's former number one Pampers brand had lost half its 70 percent market share since the 1970s, and its former number one Ivory brand made up only 5 percent of the market, bowing to Unilever's Dove, which owned four times as much of the market.[6]

"In some ways P&G's success has been its undoing," wrote Katrina Brooker. "Because its brands have been so dominant for so long, the company's culture acquired a pervasive, slavish adherence to precedent. P&G has kept going by simply . . . coming up with newer, improved versions of the same old products. Tide, for example, has gone through more than 60 product upgrades since its launch. But repeating the same formula works for only so long. The corporate landscape is littered with fallen giants of the '60s and '70s that have failed to change, to adapt: Think of Kellogg, Sears, or Kodak."[7]

Jager was adamant that rapid restructuring and cultural change were necessary to free innovation from the many layers of bureaucracy. He cited P&G's failure to launch products globally from the start, naming its clothes freshener Febreze as a prime example. At the time, it was being introduced in the

U.S. but only slowly outside the States. Jager insisted, "The product should have been launched globally in the first place. 'If we had done that, we would be launching this product around the world at the same time we were expanding it in the U.S. And we'd be realizing perhaps $500 million in sales instead of our current projection ($200 million in the U.S.).'"[8]

Jager was dead-on in theory—one he shared with P&G's board and most shareholders. Structural and cultural change was necessary to survive. However, he was way off track in the application of the theory.

WHEN CHANGE GOES TOO FAR, TOO FAST

Like a giant oak, a century-and-a-half-old company has roots that must be unearthed carefully. While similar moves were necessary to revive P&G, the pace and nature at which it was done was just as critical. This was where Jager's need for speed was more of a weakness than a strength.

"To innovate, you have to go away from the norm," maintained Jager. "You have to be rebellious or nonconventional. You have to do things differently."[9] And do things differently he did—too differently, too quickly.

Seeking to force innovation to the forefront and drive new brands to the global market rapidly, Jager, a mere nine months into the job, announced he was eliminating 13 percent of the workforce. He then disregarded business managers responsible for current products and transferred their responsibilities to global brand managers. He simultaneously established "innovation teams" that displaced the company's best and brightest from important daily roles to the ongoing development and launching of the best new brands.[10]

Jager boasted that his actions were in the spirit of "looking for rebels, for people who are willing to stick their neck out and go with their gut rather than with some rule book."[11] In effect, Jager was uprooting the giant oak, chopping off branches, and jamming it back into the ground before the soil could be prepared. The move didn't take.

Jager banked P&G's future on the liberation of the innovative rebels he knew existed in P&G's pool of more than one hundred thousand employees. He found some—but not nearly enough to wage a successful rebellion. In hindsight, perhaps even his followers were not completely loyal to their leader's marching orders. His cultural coup turned against him.

BusinessWeek's Robert Berner wrote, "When Jager took over in January 1999, he was hell-bent on it [revolutionizing a bastion of corporate conservatism]—with disastrous results. He introduced expensive new products that never caught on while letting existing brands drift. He wanted to buy two huge pharmaceutical companies, a plan that threatened P&G's identity but never was carried out . . . The family began to turn against its leader."[12]

In June 2000, seventeen months after they made him their man, the Procter board pressured Jager to resign in what Berner called "a boardroom coup unprecedented in P&G's history."[13] In their public announcement on June 8, the board also disclosed to Wall Street that fourth-quarter earnings would not meet expectations, nor would the following year's results. The board replaced Jager with P&G veteran A. G. Lafley.

QUICKLY OFF COURSE

As a chief executive, Jager failed by overfocusing the company's resources on generating the next big idea and introducing products that *Time* magazine's Daniel Eisenberg and Daren Fonda noted "left customers yawning,"[14] while underinvesting in the development and marketing of established brands. Under his tenure, sales and market share declined in sixteen of P&G's thirty key product categories, including core brands such as Crest, Pringles, and Tide. At the same time, commodity prices were increasing and currency prices shifted unfavorably, further diminishing earnings.

Less than a year into his job, "morale was sliding," explained Eisenberg and Fonda. "An overly aggressive, ill-timed restructuring program left a good number of P&G's 110,000 employees in new jobs, disoriented and distracted."[15]

As a leader, Jager failed in a much deeper way. While there were glaring, fiscally tangible reasons for Jager's short and unsuccessful tenure—he missed earnings projections twice in six months, and the company's price per share declined 52 percent—his ultimate derailers were less tangible failures of character.

There is no doubt Durk Jager faced a tough task. Restructuring the embedded culture of a 160-year-old legendary company was a massive challenge. But the challenge required more than structural change. Change can be orchestrated respectfully and incrementally, but it was not Jager's way. He went about the change forcefully and immediately, and his actions showed a gross disregard for P&G's existing culture. But more than that, his approach displayed a disregard for the lives his demands were affecting.

NOT JUST ONE REASON
FOR HIS DERAILMENT

Jager clearly displayed all of the four categories of derailers. Throughout his tenure, he maintained an intense—even feared—degree of arrogance. He openly despised the old mores of the company, making it clear that he found P&G's culture to be intolerable and wholly to blame for the company's problems. This trait he demonstrated through his oft-quoted motto, "If it ain't broke, break it."

"Jager's greatest failing," noted *Business Week*'s Berner, "was his scorn for the family. . . . [He] pitted himself against the P&G culture, contending that it was burdensome and insufferable, says Susan E. Arnold, president of P&G's beauty and feminine care division. Some go-ahead employees even wore buttons that read 'Old World/New World' to express disdain for P&G's past. 'I never wore one,' Arnold sneers. 'The old Procter is bad, and the new world is good. That didn't work.'"[16]

Jager also cultivated a ruthless image in an attempt to convey his hard-charging commitment toward turning the company around. The inauthentic veneer intimidated employees and implanted an intended sense of insecurity about their place in the company. Such actions showed "nothing is sacred," according to an unnamed source in *Marketing Week*.[17]

Rather than drive change through courageous empowerment and wise deployment of skills, Jager, a large man "built like a linebacker,"[18] attempted to force change through a fearful façade of constant bullying. The moniker "Crazy Man Durk" arose largely because he appeared to be unapproachable and irrational. He wouldn't listen to employees, was aloof to cultural concerns, and was openly critical. Jager was proud of it all. He naively believed it would win over the people's confidence in his work. "Jager will tell you himself," wrote CNN's Brooker, "the nasty things people say about him: 'I break knee caps. I make heads roll.' Once, in a meeting, a P&G insider recalls, when a colleague droned on for too long, Jager snapped: 'What kind of sh- - are you trying to clutter my mind with here?'"[19] Jager seemed to delight in making enemies.

Jager's antagonist role ultimately kept him from aligning his people with his vision. "He flunked at engaging the people of P&G," wrote *Business Week*'s John Byrne.[20] This demonstrated a blatant ignorance of the primary importance of buy-in to the success of organizations. It seemed Jager truly believed people would see that the end would justify the means.

The problem was that Jager's means were so volatile and contemptible that employees began to choose silence over truth. When the leader twice announced earnings projections far in excess of the actual numbers, analysts concluded quickly that he had been kept out of the loop about P&G's failing initiatives. Members of the organization would not speak truth to power.

In the end, the simplest cause and effect is that Jager conveyed an abject distrust of his people grounded in a flagrant overestimation of his own leadership. As a result, his people did not trust him. One source cites an episode in which the company, under Jager's leadership, tapped the phones of three staffers suspected of revealing insider information.[21] Word spread and Jager's end was near. The dilapidated bridge of leadership had finally broken, and the only repair was to replace the bridge.

Although Jager's successor, A. G. Lafley, did not name

names, he appeared to renounce the ousted leader's approach to management of change. "Speed is not a substitute for good business sense."[22]

Jager's derailment teaches us a further lesson: neither speed nor good business sense are substitutes for good leadership.

PROFILE # 4
STEVEN HEYER

"What makes a man walk away from $35 million?
That is the question that still hangs over Steven Heyer." [1]
—ALAN MURRAY of the *Wall Street Journal*
in an April 11, 2007, article

When it came time for its founding CEO, Barry Sternlicht, to transition from the day-to-day, Starwood Hotels & Resorts Worldwide sought a leader with the marketing prowess to keep its brands, including the prestigious W, Westin, and St. Regis hotels, on the upswing. It was a young, entrepreneurial company that needed an innovative leader with both business and branding experience. Steven Heyer, president and COO of Coca-Cola, appeared the perfect fit.

Nicknamed "The Tank" in college for his relentless ways, Heyer embedded a reputation as a prolific mass marketer. [2] Prior to Coca-Cola, he had served as president and COO of Turner Broadcasting System, where he was responsible for entertainment and news networks such as TBS, TNT, CNN, and their sub-brands. During his tenure at Turner, Heyer launched fourteen new television networks and introduced nineteen distinct Web sites for its CNN, Cartoon Network, and Turner Classic Movie brands.

Before Turner, Heyer was president and COO of Young &

Rubicom Advertising Worldwide and had previously spent fifteen years at Booz Allen Hamilton, ultimately becoming senior vice president and managing partner.

After Heyer was passed over for the CEO position at Coca-Cola, Starwood swooped in on their man. There was no arguing Heyer's vast experience and string of success. He was widely considered a master marketer and the perfect CEO to lead what Marc Falcone, lodging analyst at Deutsche Bank, called Starwood's "outstanding selection of brands" into the future. "Who better to guide the direction and leverage the strength of those brands than . . . Steven Heyer?"[3]

Heyer had a big vote of confidence from the top down. Founding CEO Sternlicht described him as the embodiment of "all we were searching for. . . . He is a seasoned operator with vast corporate experience on a global scale across multiple consumer businesses. He is a marketer who has championed some of the world's most valuable and global brands. He is an innovator who conceived, crafted and cultivated countless new products and partnerships over his career. My vision for Starwood was to build a culture maniacally focused on the customer and a revenue/profitability driven enterprise. Steve will help us achieve these goals."[4]

On October 1, 2004, Steven Heyer rolled into Starwood ready to showcase yet another compelling executive campaign. Unfortunately, the master marketer made a very basic marketing blunder: he failed to keep up appearances. Namely, his own.

THE RISE AND FALL OF A REPUTATION

As was his protocol, Heyer went right to polishing the branding side of the Starwood business. Within a year, he hired ex-Coca-

Cola and P&G executive Javier Benito to be his chief marketing officer, signed a deal with Creative Artists Agency to "to weave brand messages into Hollywood product," and launched the "aloft" brand, a hip younger sister of the W Hotels brand. [5] Heyer also "forged multiple lucrative advertising partnerships with companies such as Yahoo!, Apple, and BMW, who were willing to shell out major bucks for access to Starwood's high-end clientele."[6]

The zealous campaigning paid off. The company's shares rose 90 percent at one point on the wings of Heyer's marketing vision. In 2006 alone, Starwood "reported a net income of $1.04 billion, up from $422 million for the year prior."[7] He was clearly doing right by fiscal standards—something he had done everywhere he had been. He seemed once again to have the Midas touch.

Yet while the hard work and heightened company image were paying dividends in the public's mind, they were doing the opposite behind the scenes. Heyer's personal image began to fade.

A major contributor was his alienated approach to governance. Heyer often wielded his magic solo, spending little time at the corporate headquarters in White Plains, New York, and opting instead to commute from his home in Atlanta. In his contract with Starwood, he was provided an Atlanta office near his home but agreed to "spend 'at least a majority' of his workdays . . . either at headquarters or on company business trips."[8] Such was not the case, as Starwood spent, in one year, $866,000 jetting Heyer between Atlanta and his various obligations.

While Heyer was turning the company brands to gold, he was losing touch with the people he was leading. It was the beginning of an internal branding issue, and Heyer was the problem product.

Prior to his tenure at Starwood, Heyer had "been known for brusque, often difficult relations with employees," reported the *Wall Street Journal.*[9] At Starwood, this had only seemed to affect Heyer's relations with former CEO Sternlicht, who eventually resigned his post as chairman in 2005 to focus on his investment firm, Starwood Capital. The effect, however, reached well outside executive walls. "While Heyer's aggressive approach and his larger-than-life persona may have beefed up the company's bottom line," explained *Forbes*'s Evelyn Rusli, "it was also rumored to turn board members against him."[10]

Then, in February 2007, the board received an anonymous letter alleging Heyer had been involved in inappropriate activity with female employees. "An outside law firm investigated the claims," explained Marcus Baram of ABC News, "and found that Heyer, who is married, had sent suggestive and provocative e-mails and text messages to an unmarried female employee . . . According to another claim, Heyer had reportedly had an inappropriate physical encounter with a female employee outside a restaurant restroom."[11]

"The board pressed Mr. Heyer to explain the large number of e-mails and text messages to and from female employees on a variety of topics outside normal working hours. They also questioned him about his hiring and promotion practices."[12] Heyer denied any wrongdoing.

"'For an anonymous letter to basically destroy a reputation would be sinful,' Mr. Heyer said. While acknowledging he can be a difficult boss, he said the chain of events set off by the letter represented the 'straw that broke the camel's back' in his increasingly poor relationship with the company."[13]

On April 12, 2007, less than three years after he was hired,

Steven Heyer resigned, claiming life was too short to exert the energy to contest with the personal allegations.[14]

For their part, the board cited issues with Heyer's management style and a general loss of confidence in his leadership. It was the corporate version of citing irreconcilable differences. Still, the public was entitled to its own opinion, and Heyer's turn-and-burn reaction damaged his image further.

A BAD CAMPAIGN

Leaders make mistakes. While they are held to a higher standard, they still have lapses in judgment. Certain mistakes, handled tactfully, willfully, and humbly, are often forgivable to the point the position of leadership is salvageable. The same mistakes avoided and handled irresponsibly—or worse, flippantly and arrogantly—often say a lot more about a leader than the mistakes ever did. This was the case with Steven Heyer.

The Starwood board had been willing to overlook Heyer's rough edges given his continued accomplishments. Yet, Heyer was flippant in his self-consumption. His lack of humility was first evident by his roguish work habits, opting to commute from his Atlanta office instead of remaining a steady presence at headquarters in White Plains. However, the real straw that broke the camel's back was Heyer's handling of the accusations.

When an accused leader denies wrongdoing, we expect him to at least campaign for his innocence—to stand behind his claims and clear his name. One has, at least, the benefit of the doubt. Heyer claimed he had done nothing wrong regarding the allegations—then ran. Given his flawless handling of every brand he had ever touched, this was a shockingly elementary marketing mistake. His quick and arcane exit was like broadcasting a scandalous political ad against himself. To the majority of onlookers it communicated only one thing: "I did it but owe no explanation."

Heyer's resignation included forgoing a large severance payment and forfeiting "stock options, unvested restricted stock and other unpaid compensation."[15] Compared to his contemporaries who took tens of millions in severance and other compensation, Heyer was getting the shaft—and accepting it.

The *Wall Street Journal*'s Alan Murray asked the question on everyone's minds: "What makes a man walk away from $35 million? That is the question that still hangs over Steven Heyer, who resigned last week as chief executive of Starwood Hotels & Resorts and voluntarily abandoned that much in severance and stock-based compensation."[16]

Continuing the prevailing thought, Reuters's Emily Chasan noted, "While other ousted CEOs, including former Hewlett-Packard Co. CEO Carly Fiorina and Home Depot CEO Bob Nardelli, walked away with multimillion-dollar severance packages, Heyer, 54, received no severance and is even forfeiting his stock options. 'Certainly boards are under pressure to create smaller severance packages,' said John Challenger, CEO of global outplacement firm Challenger Gray & Christmas. 'There was likely something else going on here . . . Who knows?'"[17]

If one considers only the financial implications of Starwood's board allowing Heyer to walk, the conclusion would be that it was a foolish decision. Heyer had exceeded the board's expectations where the business was concerned; his boosting of Starwood's brands led to a doubling of its net income.[18] But there *was* something else going on, and this other factor was more critical to the success of the business than the profits.

WHAT LESSON WAS THERE TO BE LEARNED—AND DID HE LEARN IT?

Heyer was a phenomenal marketer, but he ultimately derailed because he was a poor leader. A leader's primary charge and his foundational role are never mutually exclusive. Even if a leader excels at the very thing for which the board hired him, if he fails to apply the foundational skills afforded by his position, then he fails overall.

Heyer's derailment ensued because he never committed himself to the role of a leader within Starwood. He grew the company, boosted the stock, and polished its brands, but he remained dangerously detached. He was a steam engine attempting to pull the rest of the train without being attached to it. While Heyer knew the company brands, he never knew the company—and the company never knew him. His detachment only exasperated the allegations of his inappropriate behavior. One can only imagine employees, upon hearing the news, uttering under their breath, "So that's what he's been doing . . . That's what kind of guy he is . . . No wonder he's been hiding out."

The people had no personal history with which to counterbalance Heyer's actions. Perhaps for many employees, the accusations were their first interaction with Heyer's personal image outside his marketing handiwork.

When Heyer walked away "with his head held high," as he indicated, it did not send the typical message. Heyer's image was not the victorious warrior leaving the battlefield with some collateral damage. In her article announcing Heyer's resignation, *Forbes*'s Evelyn Rusli summed this up well. "Steven J. Heyer," she asserted, "still hasn't learned to play nice."[19] In the end, it seemed the marketing master could enhance the appearance of everything but himself.

The business world will now watch with considerable interest to see if Steven Heyer, now chairman at Next3D, has learned from his mistakes. It's a safe bet he will succeed in making household names out of his new company's brands. But will he remember to lead?

PROFILE # 5
FRANK RAINES

"Neither Mr. Raines nor Mr. Howard, nor anyone from their staffs, investigated these concerns or took corrective action. Thus, the practices I had identified continued, and I faced continuing reprisal for raising concerns about these issues."[1]

—ROGER BARNES, whistleblower
former Fannie Mae accountant

In the late 1990s, middle-class homeownership looked to be peaking after nearly a decade-long run of good fortune for any company in the mortgage business, especially for the government-chartered and -sponsored Fannie Mae. Under chief executive James A. Johnson, the value of its assets had tripled, and its share price had risen sevenfold.

When Johnson left his office for the last time in December 1998, Fannie Mae faced the challenge of sustaining its run of double-digit growth and its reputation as the "dominant force in the mortgage industry."[2] To do so, it would need to rely on creative, non-traditional efforts to expand the housing market through "groups—black and Hispanic families, immigrants and single people—that traditionally have been far less likely to buy houses."[3]

Fannie Mae needed a leader who not only understood all sides of the government-backed mortgage business but also understood the people who would become their most important customers. Franklin Delano Raines seemed perfectly suited.

The son of two janitors and one of seven children, Raines understood the magnitude of home ownership, having watched his father piecemeal together a house from scratch over five years. His parents "never earned more than $15,000 a year, yet his father managed to leave behind $300,000 when he died," thanks largely to his scrappy investment in their home. "Raines remarked, 'It's a dramatic demonstration of how important access to capital and homeownership are in the lives of working-class people.'"[4]

Raines leveraged the work ethic and financial wisdom passed down from his parents into a noteworthy career. After graduating from Harvard College, Harvard Law School, and Magdalen College at Oxford as a Rhodes Scholar, he quickly gained a reputation for tight accounting, results-driven leadership, and shrewd diplomacy, simultaneously climbing the political, legal, and corporate ladders and working in varying capacity with the Nixon, Carter, and Clinton administrations.

"As director of the White House's Office of Management and Budget," wrote the *New York Times*'s Richard Stevenson in a 1998 article, "he was often the point man for the Administration in political and policy battles with the Republican leadership in Congress, including the successful negotiations last year on a plan to balance the Federal budget."[5]

At forty-nine, Raines possessed the whole package, and there was no reason to believe he would not continue his run at the controls of the nation's most central mortgage-based company.

On January 1, 1999, he became the CEO of Fannie Mae—the first African American CEO of a Fortune 500 corporation and the unofficial key master of the American dream.

NEWTON'S LAW: WHAT GOES UP . . .

From the outset, everything climbed upward, including Raines's earnings. "As chairman and CEO of Fannie Mae," explained a *Business Week* article, "Raines helped turn it into a financial behemoth . . . The price of Fannie's stock soared during his tenure, and Raines earned roughly $90 million in salary and bonuses."[6]

With Raines conducting, Fannie Mae not only sustained double-digit income growth but vastly expanded its reach with new technology and products. The biggest—and costliest—of Fannie's expansions was Raines's commitment to invest $2 trillion in mortgage programs that would make homeownership and rental housing more affordable for eighteen million more families. "Raines began a pilot program in 1999 to issue bank loans to individuals with low to moderate income, and to ease credit requirements on loans that Fannie Mae purchased from banks. Raines promoted the program saying that it would allow consumers who were 'a notch below what our current underwriting has required' to get home loans."[7] The program included sub-prime mortgages.

This greater opportunity of homeownership, Raines believed, was Fannie Mae's mission personified. He was hailed a hero by many.

The work was not without challenges, however, as Fannie was constantly under attack from mortgage industry rivals who insisted the company maintained an unfair advantage with its government ties and under-regulated procedures. Raines rose to each challenge with the nimble diplomacy for which he was known. He became "a master at the art of wielding an iron fist inside a velvet glove," asserted an article in *BusinessWeek* in 2002. "With charm, impeccable connections, and understated arm-twisting, he repeatedly staves off attacks by industry rivals determined to blunt what they believe is an unfair advantage stemming from Fannie's quasi-public status."[8]

. . . MUST COME DOWN

There was one attack, however, for which Raines was neither prepared nor deft enough to defeat.

From 1999 to 2002, Fannie Mae accountant Roger Barnes sent repeated correspondence to "a wide range of Fannie Mae managers and executives,"[9] including Frank Raines and Fannie CFO Timothy Howard, urging them to look into accounting irregularities he had discovered. Barnes noted that the amortization of certain expenses, "a key element in Fannie's profitability, was . . . being manipulated to meet earnings targets."[10]

When Barnes's concerns were repeatedly disregarded or inadequately considered, he left the company in November 2003, claiming his hand was forced by "threats, intimidation and reprisal" against him and others who raised concerns about the company's accounting.[11] Barnes also noted "the atmosphere and culture . . . is one of intimidation, restraint of dissenting opinions and pressure to be part of the team."[12]

The following year, Barnes, no longer silenced by Fannie attorneys, went public with his concerns, blowing the whistle on the mortgage giant in a twenty-six-page statement to the Subcommittee on Capital Markets, Insurance and Government Sponsored Enterprises of the U.S. House of Representatives Committee on Financial Services. He described "a three-year effort to convince senior Fannie management, including chief executive Franklin D. Raines and Chief Financial Officer J. Timothy Howard, that the company's system for accounting . . . was seriously flawed."[13]

Barnes was subsequently asked to meet with investigators at the Securities and Exchange Commission and the Department of Justice. An investigation by the Office of Federal Housing Enterprise Oversight (OFHEO), the federal agency that oversees Fannie Mae, ensued.

The glaring paradox was that during his tenure at Fannie, Raines remained a proponent of the high standards to which all leaders of large corporations must adhere. For example, while testifying about the infamous collapse of Enron Corp., "Raines once asserted: 'It is wholly irresponsible and unacceptable for corporate leaders to say they did not know—or suggest it is not their duty to know—about the operations and activities of their company, particularly when it comes to risks that threaten the fundamental viability of their company.'"[14]

Two years later during a July 2003 interview concerning the Freddie Mac (Fannie's smaller government-sponsored rival) accounting scandal, Raines was asked if the improprieties at Freddie would result in a loss of Fannie Mae's federal advantages. Answered Raines, "What Fannie Mae does is important to the country and to homebuyers. And we do it, I think, very well. And as long as those two things are true, I don't expect Congress will take any action."[15]

Had one noted his noncommittal posturing in that response—"I think . . . as long as those things are true . . . I don't expect . . ."—one might have concluded Raines was withholding something, acting perhaps a bit *too* diplomatic for even his track record.

One year later he would shift his commentary on the standards of leadership from denoting nothing to defending the practices that threatened the legacy of his successful run at Fannie.

On September 17, 2004, two weeks after Roger Barnes took his allegations public, a report by the OFHEO revealed Fannie had in fact used illegal accounting methods and misstated its earnings. The SEC's chief accountant confirmed the violations, which included the one Barnes cited in his testimony.

COMING OFF THE TRACKS

It is said that adverse circumstances do not make or break you; they reveal you. It is a fitting maxim given Raines's telling response to the OFHEO's confirmation of illegal accounting. His unwillingness to accept responsibility revealed his three primary derailers: 1) a lack of authenticity, 2) a lack of humility, and 3) a lack of courage.

Testifying before a House subcommittee, Raines spun the illegal accounting activity into a charmingly ambiguous prose that spanned from victimhood to accountability and back again. "These accounting standards are highly complex and require determinations over which experts often disagree," Raines insisted.[16]

Stephen Labaton in the *New York Times* elaborated, "Breaking his silence two weeks after a report by the company's main regulator plunged the management of the mortgage giant

into crisis by accusing senior executives of manipulating accounting and earnings to get bigger bonuses, Mr. Raines said the federal agency had drawn unfair conclusions. He said the agency
denied the company a fair hearing and inexplicably waged an
unusually public campaign against it." Yet, "'I want to make one
thing very clear,' Mr. Raines said, departing from his prepared
text. 'I've tried my best to make sure we've done the right thing
in the right way.' If he is proved wrong, 'our board and our shareholders will hold me accountable,' he said. 'I will hold myself
accountable.'"[17]

Yet for all his responsible remarks, Raines's steadfast accountability shed into steadfast stubbornness when he resigned less
than three months after the scandal surfaced, taking with him a
$19 million severance package. When he stood firm behind the
illegal accounting even while he and two other executives "agreed
to pay $24.7 million, including a $2 million fine, to settle a civil
lawsuit filed in December 2006," the reasons for his derailment
were solidified. The AP also reported that "Raines was forced to
give up Fannie Mae stock options valued at $15.6 million as part
of the settlement."[18]

The discrepancy between the legal conclusions and Raines's
vague posturing sends the wrong message: the leader is larger
than both the company and the bodies that govern the company's practices. Whether Raines understood it as such is
debatable. Perhaps he was not entirely aware of the illegal
nature of the practices he was allowing. Perhaps he does believe
certain accounting measures are relative to circumstances. Still,
one thing cannot be debated: Raines had and still has every
opportunity to admit, in the very least, to poor judgment, lax
standards, or subjective governance. He has admitted none,

stepping only slightly above the abject denial he spoke so adamantly against in his contemporaries at Enron. "I previously stated that I would hold myself accountable if the SEC determined that significant mistakes were made in the company's accounting. By my early retirement, I have held myself accountable."[19]

His "accountable" actions were so well spun into ambiguity that one is left to conclude at best that Raines was withholding something. Was stepping down a clear confession? Hardly. And Raines was shrewd enough to know it. Stepping down was only a hazy concession.

THE PROBLEMS CONTINUE

The great irony is that Fannie Mae was chartered by Congress in 1938 to provide liquidity and stability to the U.S. housing and mortgage markets. Since the brief reign of Frank Raines, Fannie has fallen well short of its charter and become one of the biggest flies in the economic ointment. One could pose an argument for laying the blame before or after Raines's tenure—and such arguments are out there—but it is difficult not to conclude that Raines's legacy is somehow less than admirable.

Reporting the Fannie Mae hearing, the *New York Times*'s Eric Dash recounted Roger Barnes's written admonition that "the culture in the controller's division was such that many employees knew or suspected that the company was regularly engaging in improper income management, and it became a joke that the controller's division could produce any income statement that the company wanted."[20]

BusinessWeek's Mike McNamee was more concise: "Fannie

Mae's chairman and CEO bet that his political prowess could protect him from an accounting scandal. He was wrong."[21]

Further, "In the five years that Mr. Raines has been at the helm, Fannie's cumulative shareholder return, including reinvested dividends, has been 4% compared with the 23% achieved by the S&P financial sector."[22]

Beyond Raines's millions in settlement requirements, Fannie Mae separately paid a $400 million civil fine in a settlement with the OFHEO and the SEC in an agreement to make top-to-bottom changes in its accounting procedures to avoid future Raines-like accounting manipulation scandals. The earnings restatement drained 40 percent of Fannie Mae's profits from 2001 to 2004.[23]

For now, Mr. Raines remains in the background where he can best minimize the mentions of his name in the same sentence with the economic turmoil that still exists. For all his shortcomings that surfaced at Fannie Mae, he still displays an exceptional ability to mollify conflict—in his silence and only when necessary, in his defense. "I left Fannie Mae in 2004," he explained, "and both Fannic Mac and its regulator have stated that the company's current financial problems are the result of mortgages purchased years after my departure."[24]

Raines certainly is not solely responsible for the collapse of the housing market we now face, but in a meeting to discuss the demise of the American economy, we would certainly want to ask Raines to weigh in on his contribution to the devastation of the housing sector in particular and the economy in general.

PROFILE # 6
DICK FULD

"As long as I am alive this firm will never be sold. And if it is sold after I die, I will reach back from the grave and prevent it."

—DICK FULD in December 2007

D ick Fuld was as insider as they come. He was equally as intense. His long and successful career at Lehman Brothers began in 1969 after his dream to become an air force pilot "came to an abrupt halt when he got into a fist fight with a commanding officer." In Fuld's defense, he was said to have been protecting a younger cadet who was being mistreated.[1]

This heart for the underdog gave rise to man who seemed unbreakable—tough-talking his way upward over a thirty-nine-year history with Lehman Brothers. Fuld was famously aggressive, uncomfortably intense, and unquestionably smart. His aura could fill a room—giving second chair to his equally impressive but less-mentioned education, military service, and numerous service positions on non-profit and professional boards.

Fuld was a force—bigger than himself. And during his ascent to the top, he became the sort of leader who could succeed on Wall Street right away—but not forever.

STRENGTH IS WEAKNESS
WELL HARNESSED

In November 2003, the man "they called . . . the Gorilla—the brawler known as the scariest man on Wall Street" took over as the chief at Lehman Brothers. There, "in a world where the top brass are generally suave . . . Fuld stood apart," wrote the *Times Online*'s Tom Bawden.[2] And it would be his rogue—and many felt, timely—strength that kept him at the top. "He exuded hostility," explained Ken Auletta, media critic for *New Yorker* magazine. "But Fuld became a favorite at the company and also played a part in keeping Lehman's name intact."[3]

Under Fuld's stewardship, Lehman soared. By 2006, *Institutional Investor* magazine had named him America's top chief executive. Companies around the world clamored for Lehman's services and personal attention from the brawler. In response to the popularity, Fuld accepted positions on everything from the Federal Reserve Bank, the Ronald McDonald House Charities, Inc., the Robin Hood Foundation, and others. By the end of 2007, he was at the pinnacle of the financial world, having turned a $102 million loss in 1993 into a $4.2 billion profit in 2007.

In March 2008, Fuld was named to *Barron's* list of the world's thirty best CEOs and dubbed "Mr. Wall Street." "Under Fuld's stewardship," explained Alice Gomstyn of ABC News, "Lehman's net income increased more than six times over . . . In one year, Fuld himself received more than $70 million in salary, stock options and other compensation, according to the compensation firm James F. Reda and Associates."[4]

Insiders were well aware of Fuld's "big" reputation, seeing

the characterization as something to be feared, admired, and even envied. Fuld "is the most intense person I've ever met in my life," said Bruce Foerster, who served as the head of Lehman's global equities syndicate from 1992 to 1994. "When he walks into a room, it's electric. He's electric."[5]

While Fuld's electricity was inspiring in the right context, it could become foolish in the wrong context. Dick "thought he could intimidate you out of losing money," one colleague confessed.[6]

The same force that made Fuld would eventually derail him. There is so little space to stand at the top, and it takes more than brute strength to stay balanced. In fact, it often requires qualities quite the opposite—patience and finesse—something the financial world would discover Fuld was lacking.

"You weren't easygoing around Dick Fuld," explained Foerster. "You took a couple of extra breaths of air before you started talking to him just so you had some extra oxygen in your brain."[7]

Oxygen in your brain and money in your pocket—it was difficult to criticize Fuld for his bullish ways when he's responsible for making so many people rich. Fuld was well aware of the wealth he inflicted on others, but stubbornly ignorant to what might happen if he made a wrong move.

Let us not forget that Fuld was a fighter for the underdog—so this type of hubris wasn't expected. And Fuld was a company man—blame him for an inflated salary, an ego, and arrogance, but don't point the finger at him for selfishness. His commitment to the success of Lehman Brothers and its shareholders was sincere. "As long as I am alive this firm will never be sold," Fuld famously told the *Wall Street Journal.*

"And if it is sold after I die, I will reach back from the grave and prevent it."[8]

The financial world would believe him, until the credit crisis came—perhaps the only force tougher than the Wall Street brawler. Markets were crashing; investors were pulling funds; and the American public was pocketing their pennies and losing their homes, their jobs, and their confidence. For the first time, Fuld was facing a fight bigger than Wall Street. It was then he made the classic competitive error: he grossly underestimated his opponent and overestimated his strength.

WEAKNESS IS
STRENGTH UNHARNESSED

In June 2008, Lehman Bothers posted a second-quarter loss of $2.8 billion, its first loss since going public in 1994. The blow was crushing to the organization, and to Fuld—the man whose track record had, for more than a decade, continued to overshadow itself year after year. Now, his first poor showing initiated the ousting of two key Lehman executives.

Fuld had been struck with a solid left hook. As he had always done before, he shook it off and fought harder. Unfortunately, Lehman had been cut bad, and forceful Fuld could not stop the bleeding.

In September 2008, Lehman reported yet another loss—this time of $3.9 billion. Days later, the firm filed for bankruptcy protection, and eventually bankruptcy—the largest in history.

Already fragile, the financial system stumbled to absorb such an impact. Fuld crumbled almost immediately.

"[He] became a symbol of failure, the face of arrogant,

blinded, massively overleveraged Wall Street," wrote Steve Fishman in *New York* magazine. "Fuld is blamed for betting the farm on the way up, then stubbornly refusing to recognize the company's dire straits on the way down. A few weeks after the bankruptcy, Congress summoned him to Washington for a deeply humiliating inquisition. 'You're the villain today,' one congressman told him."[9]

For the first time in his life, Dick Fuld the fighter did not pick the fight. Perhaps that is why he refused to give in—even when it was clear Lehman was bleeding out. He had been bullied by a force bigger than his own, and it seemed he would rather die fighting than find a way to survive and fight another day.

"It wasn't for lack of trying that Lehman crashed and burned," reported the *New York Post*. "In the firm's last days, CEO Dick Fuld turned first to GE's Jeff Immelt, then to AIG's Marty Sullivan, for help. Fuld had hoped Immelt would take as much as a 20 percent stake in Lehman in order to quiet the then-mounting questions surrounding Lehman's toxic $630 billion balance sheet. Immelt, however, opted to take a pass."[10]

Lehman Brothers staff members have reported that after the downfall Fuld was "broken and shell-shocked. He has lost a fortune, but for such an ambitious man, the biggest loss is to his pride."[11] The money he lost—for himself and many others—tested his pride at every level. Perhaps the biggest test of pride was also the most visible sign that Fuld had fallen from grace—his forced exit from the office he called home. He "was 'banished' from his corner office in Lehman's Seventh Avenue headquarters and instead moved to a Sixth Avenue building, where he and other Lehman executives who weren't offered jobs at Barclays [the global financial services provider who purchased

Lehman's good assets] will continue to work through Lehman's bankruptcy proceedings."[12]

While it's easy to respect the strength of a man like Fuld, one has to also take into account that such strength is a weakness when it cannot be harnessed. Ultimately, it was Fuld's intensity-turned-stubborn-arrogance that did him in.

ON TRIAL IN THE COURT
OF PUBLIC OPINION

Bruised and broken, the public trials of Dick Fuld began—bringing the high-dollar, high-stakes truths of Wall Street into living rooms everywhere. Fuld, still appearing baffled by the reality of the situation, shockingly appears again in character—denying any wrongdoing and fighting until the end. He still had not learned the lesson.

"The lack of regulatory framework contributed to where we are today," Fuld said during testimony covered by C-SPAN. "I am not proud of the fact that I lost that much money, but it does show that our compensation system did work. I firmly believed that we would get back on the road to profitability and recover."[13]

While his intentions may have been pure, most agree that Dick Fuld's derailment resulted from two things: 1) he refused to quit fighting, and 2) he failed to size up his opponent.

"His failure goes beyond refusing to make a trade that he did not like," notes John Gapper of the *Financial Times*. He "displayed confusion and ambiguity about how to address the credit crisis . . . The investment bank suffered from not conveying a clear message either internally or externally. His fall was classic, downright Shakespearean. A tragedy. At least a business-school case study."[14]

Killer instincts, an aggressive persona, and a scrappy thirty-nine-year climb to the top made Dick Fuld the prime candidate to sit in the leadership chair at one of the world's most prestigious financial institutions. He was confident, intimidating, and smart. However, confidence, arrogance, and even proximity blinded Fuld from seeing any potential downfall, or any signs of weakness—in himself or Lehman. By the time he realized he was fighting a losing battle, it was too late—Dick Fuld had already been knocked out.

DERAILMENT IN
SLOW MOTION

DE-
RAILED

DERAILMENT IS A PROCESS

First pride, then the crash—the bigger the ego, the harder the fall.[1]

—SOLOMON

M ost of us can only imagine being in a train wreck. The concussion of impact, the wrenching sounds of twisting metal and shattering glass, the terrifying screams of passengers, the moans of the injured and dying. Some experts believe as many as eight hundred passengers lost their lives in the worst train wreck in history.[2] On June 6, 1981, in Bihar, India, seven out of the nine cars plunged from a bridge into the Bagmati River. The reasons for this disaster are convoluted. A cyclone in the area made the tracks excessively wet and caused flash flooding in and around the river. The conditions made it impossible for rescue workers to reach the area in a timely manner. Although first responders found several hundred bodies, most were never recovered.

The real cause of this disaster was that the engineer slammed on the train's brakes to avoid hitting a cow.[3] We will never know exactly how this tragedy actually occurred and can only speculate as to the real reasons. Maybe the hot, humid conditions made the engineer drowsy. Perhaps he was not exercising adequate caution under the worst imaginable conditions. Or he could have been preoccupied replaying a recent argument with his wife. But suddenly a "sacred animal" appears in the watery haze, and he overreacts, plunging the crowded rail cars into the swollen river.

Derailments of leaders can be equally hard to sort out. Certainly each of the leaders' downfalls described in the preceding chapters involves a complex set of reasons and circumstances. We see the headlines, watch the news coverage, and read the voyeuristic details of their demise. The smoldering piles of wreckage mark ruined companies, ruined careers, ruined reputations. It looks as if the crash took place in one cataclysmic instant—one wrong turn and then the screeching sound of twisting metal—a massive derailment. It is not the whole story.

Derailment occurs over time—it really happens *before* the crash. An ignored warning signal . . . the inattention to feedback, and one wrong turn leads to another. The force of momentum in the wrong direction is strong enough that the train leaves the two parallel steel rails. It's just that the consequences are more apparent after the crash—the damage and casualties.

Derailment occurs with a crescendo of intensity. If we saw it happening, it would perhaps be like seeing in slow motion a train approaching a washed-out bridge. We would want to yell and wave at the engineer to hit the brakes before it was too late—but would he hear us? Perhaps he would simply ignore us.

DERAILMENT IS A PROCESS

The six profiles in the previous chapters are a veritable treasure for seeing and understanding how derailment happens and how we stay on track. Their six slow-motion train wrecks provide wisdom for those who don't want to meet the same demise.

Derailment occurs in a predictable progression—a process that those who derail seem to follow. Derailed leaders progress through five stages as they head toward their demise. Perhaps there's hope for us to learn about these escalating stages of derailment and stay on track.

While derailment is a progression, circumstances can also have an impact. In the Bihar train wreck, the cow happened to be standing at the precise location that when the engineer slammed on the brakes, the passenger cars had nowhere to fall but into the river. The ill-timed cyclone dumped a huge volume of water into the surrounding territory, making the river more treacherous. While mitigating circumstances certainly played a role, the engineer was still at the epicenter of the tragedy. His decisions and reactions to the circumstances ultimately put the train in the river.

STAGE I: A FAILURE OF SELF-/OTHER-AWARENESS

Being self-aware gives us insight into our own desires, hopes, motives, feelings, and moods. Derailed leaders seem to often manifest a lack of self-awareness, as though they view themselves through a foggy mirror. Self-awareness is a prerequisite for managing ourselves well—the subject of a later chapter on self-management.

Derailed leaders also seem to lack awareness of and concern for others. This type of insight informs us as to the needs, desires, hopes, and moods of others that we might respond appropriately. It involves empathy, consideration, and general attentiveness to the interests of others. Derailed leaders seem oblivious to the impact of their behavior on others and of the resulting failure to build a strong, aligned team. They also fail to see themselves as others do—to take into account that others will relate to them on the basis of those perceptions. This type of interpersonal calibration requires understanding and humility.

Despite Carly Fiorina's stellar track record of success—and popularity—when it came time to lead the giant engine of Hewlett-Packard, she displayed an errant overconfidence in her ability to run the train solo. She needed others but didn't appear to know it. She lacked insight in both self- and other-awareness. She first failed to see her own limitations—that she could not successfully lead H-P without the support and alignment of others. She also failed to judge how her independence would alienate the very people she needed to succeed.

When Compaq head Michael Capellas resigned just weeks after the merger with H-P, Fiorina refused to replace him with a new COO. She also limited executives' and managers' control, insisting all significant decisions channel through her office. She was a strong force but not nearly strong enough to keep the huge H-P train on the right tracks. She did not see it then—and still does not, it seems, see it now.

Did Bob Nardelli honestly believe Home Depot employees would follow a leader who had nine private parking spaces and a private elevator to his office where he could electronically peer over everyone's shoulder from his private enclave? Those who derail often seem to lack a sense of how to treat others—there's no interpersonal inner plumb line that guides them. Like

Fiorina, Jager, and Nardelli, they fail to see within themselves the rattling of their own demise.

STAGE II—HUBRIS: PRIDE
BEFORE THE FALL

As kids we didn't like the know-it-alls in our classrooms, and we don't like them in the workforce either. Hubris—extreme arrogance—manifests itself in two ways. You see it in the leader who believes he or she is the epicenter of an organization's success.

Despite Home Depot's storied entrepreneurial, fraternal culture, Nardelli presumed his controlling methodology was better. Instead of using the positive momentum within Home Depot's culture, he cut loose from the culture entirely and bled the orange-blooded faithful to death. Nardelli did not seek out the wisdom of the two legendary founders, Arthur Blank and Bernie Marcus, who created Home Depot's culture. When Blank was asked how many times Nardelli arranged lunch with him, he replied, "None."[4] It was hubris that kept Nardelli from drafting on the knowledge and wisdom of the men who made Home Depot so successful.

In stark contrast, Lou Gerstner, the fabled chairman and CEO of IBM, who orchestrated the behemoth technology company's turnaround, said, "The thing I have learned at IBM is that culture is everything."[5] Gerstner was known for exemplifying the humility to learn from the organization he was responsible for leading. He insisted on this culture at IBM. Gerstner chronicled IBM's turnaround in his book *Who Says Elephants Can't Dance?*, which he dedicated to "the thousands of IBMers who never gave up on their company, their colleagues and themselves."[6] Jim

Collins pointed out that "in the end, Gerstner was clearly ambitious for IBM first and foremost, beyond himself."[7]

Reality dictates that no matter how bright and capable a leader might be, the work of the organization must be accomplished by trusted colleagues. A leader's inference that he or she is primarily responsible for the organization's success demonstrates blatant hubris. This very attitude suggests that the leader feels he is above everyone else and that he believes other people have less value. Jager's disrespect of P&G's longstanding culture and his general dismissiveness of others set himself up for failure.

STAGE III—MISSED EARLY WARNING SIGNALS

Like the California train engineer who ignored blatant warning signals while texting on his cell phone, the early warning signals of derailment were there for all six leaders but not heeded. People were yelling and waving their hands, but these engineers paid no attention. In their arrogance, they missed the signals.

Dick Fuld was born a winner, yet he was so focused on winning the financial prize that he failed to see the chasm into which he was guiding Lehman. He had tunnel vision.

Fiorina's mishandling of Walter Hewlett and the Compaq merger was only symbolic of the bigger problem: she was overcontrolling and refused to trust others with the work of the organization. According to the H-P board, she lacked operations expertise and needed help. But she would not have it. The big warning signals Fiorina missed were the board's repeated recommendations that she spread the leadership responsibility—the clear implication being that she needed more operational expertise to get H-P earnings back up.[8]

These otherwise talented leaders did not see the warning signals represented by subtle but persistent feedback about their own inner states, others' diminishing confidence in them, or the wrong direction in which they were leading the company. Early warning signals should have jarred their attention to avoid the danger ahead. Instead, our profiled leaders barreled ahead toward the inevitable crash. Board members, colleagues, and even the media provided signals that should have alerted them to hit the brakes before it was too late. They simply did not heed the warnings.

STAGE IV—RATIONALIZING

When it becomes apparent to a leader that he is losing the confidence of colleagues or a board, his or her defenses are heightened. A siege mentality takes over, and the leader begins to rationalize his actions. Stage IV further insulates him from the very information that could either fend off disaster or greatly limit the damage.

In Stage III the leader ignored the feedback. In Stage IV the leader twists data to fit his view of the world. In an attempt to maintain his psychological equilibrium, the derailing leader believes he is right and must stay the course, despite many warning signals to the contrary.

While a salvage operation might still be possible, the leader focuses solely on personal preservation. She deflects blame, denies responsibility, accuses others of jealousy or ambition— anything to avoid accepting personal responsibility. She assumes the role of victim.

In this frame of mind, leaders can do some very stupid things. In a stunning display of obtuseness, Nardelli held a stockholder's meeting and asked the board to not attend. Those attending the meeting were given very limited time to ask questions. Nardelli battened the hatches perhaps to avoid having to answer for Home Depot's dismal stock performance and his personal compensation. He refused to be bothered by people he felt were in the way of his success. In truth, he was putting up taller and taller defenses. In the end, the walls he erected caved in on him.

Within a year of her dismissal from H-P, Fiorina released a memoir that did little but rationalize her dismissal by blaming her underestimation of other people's insecurity and lack of trustworthiness. We can only speculate about what might have happened if Fiorina had displayed a respect for H-P's culture and humbly sought the help of trusted advisors to manage the company.

STAGE V—DERAILMENT

The emissary comes to the leader's office and says, "I'm sorry . . . it's over. We all had high hopes for you here, but we need to help you leave in a way that preserves the company and maintains your dignity." An irony of Stage V is that despite the board's actions to preserve their CEO's dignity, our six profiled leaders undid this preservation of dignity with his or her own actions. This is the stage where we read and hear about it in the business media. We count the bodies and try to clean up the wreckage.

Probably on a less grand scale, we nonetheless will face the same challenges as our profiled leaders in the previous six chapters. We do not have to be one of those slow motion train wrecks! We may never be in this situation involving cataclysmic meetings with boards or the loss of billions of dollars of stockholder value, but every day we will experience the need to stay on track—the subject of the following chapters.

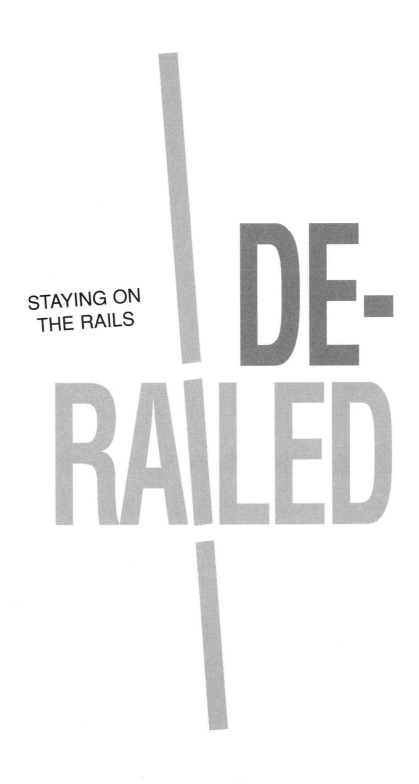

STAYING ON
THE RAILS

DE-
RAILED

WHAT'S YOUR CHARACTER QUOTIENT?

"I think I've been a great citizen."[1]
—O. J. SIMPSON

It seemed the perfect getaway. Anne and I desperately needed one of those "be alone, be quiet" retreats away from work, travel, and the stress of daily life. Close friends loaned us their cabin in the Appalachian Mountains. Marcie, our boys' star baby-sitter, agreed to stay with them for the long weekend. Everything appeared perfect. We arrived at the beautiful log cabin nestled in a forest of old oaks with a dramatic front-porch view of stacked mountain ranges. I picked out a rocker, and my blood pressure started to reflect the peace of my surroundings. I had to check to make sure I had a pulse. "This is good," I said to Anne.

We apparently were out of cell phone range during the last part of the drive up, so my phone didn't ring. But three calls had come in the last half hour—one from home and two from the office—which caused my blood pressure to rebound quickly. I called home first. Marcie answered and said, "The boys are fine, but your office really needs to talk with you." She mentioned the name of a coworker and said, "He's been arrested and charged with a felony."

As I sat in stunned silence, my mind flashed quickly to this man—a highly respected senior statesman of our profession, an elder in his church, a frequent volunteer to inner-city missions, a father of two, married to his college sweetheart, a survivor of a World War II POW camp, an outstanding amateur photographer, and a trusted colleague at work. I simply could not get my brain wrapped around this devastating news—I had no categories to explain this unbelievable anomaly. The taped news reports I saw later of him being led away in handcuffs put my denial system into overdrive, but his eventual sentencing to a North Carolina federal prison removed any doubt about this man's double life.

THE WELL OF CHARACTER

Historically, psychologists labeled individuals with socially maladaptive behaviors as "character disordered." Their problems resulted from a defect in their "character." We all have a few loose nuts and bolts in our psyches, but, as in my colleague's case, some can be quite serious. Life is full to the brim with opportunities for good or evil—our character determines which way we go. While we are not discussing behavior in our jobs that sends us to jail, actions that marginalize us or get us fired emanate from the same well . . . the well of character.

We always become who we are. It may take time or stress or illness, but what's inside us tends to come out. Our character serves as the wellspring from which our behavior emerges. Os Guinness confirms this:

Character . . . is the essential "stuff" a person is made of, the inner reality and quality in which thoughts, speech, decision, behavior, and relations are rooted. As such, character determines behavior just as behavior demonstrates character.[2]

It's not unusual for today's leaders to be charismatic and to have a penchant for celebrity. Many receive media training—how to look good and sound good on the cable business shows. It's perfectly appropriate for a leader to learn to communicate effectively in the media, but character must outweigh charisma. Character is not about personal charm and appeal. Sound character works like a boat's ballast, so that when we encounter turbulence, we don't keel over and take on water. If we are top heavy and place more emphasis on having a vivacious personality, dressing for success, or having a slick presentation than on having substance, we are eventually going to sink.

Character is not about intelligence. As David Gergen has pointed out, if intelligence and character were the same, Presidents Nixon and Clinton would have been two of the best. Neither controlled their passions. Gergen added, "Capacity counts, but once a candidate passes that test, character counts even more."[3] In the past few years we have seen a tremendous number of government officials being investigated for a variety of criminal acts and violations of the public trust. Many of these individuals score high on IQ but low on CQ (Character Quotient)—they are character-challenged.

In our post-modern, media-saturated world, it seems to not matter whether people make statements that are objectively true as long as the messenger acts hip and cool. As Bret Stephens wrote recently in the *Wall Street Journal*, "Modern culture has severed many of the remaining links between merit and celebrity. We make a fetish of uninteresting, detestable, loud or unaccomplished people: Paris Hilton, Princess Di, Keith Olbermann, Michael Jackson."[4] A visitor to the United States might well read the headlines and conclude that this society values personality more than the personal qualities of honesty and integrity in its leaders. In fact, character is the foundation of great leadership. We have to get this right to stay on track.

THE CHARACTER OF THE LEADER

Leaders must set direction, gain alignment among diverse constituencies, risk change, build high-performing teams, achieve results, go the extra mile, and endure ungodly stress. To be enthusiastically followed, leaders must also be guided by an inner compass that fosters trust on the part of their followers.

How does character guide a leader's behavior? As Os Guinness states so well:

> Externally, character provides the point of trust that links leaders with followers. Internally, character is the part-gyroscope, part-brake that provides the leader's deepest source of bearings and strongest source of restraint. In many instances the first prompting to do good and the last barrier against doing wrong are the same—character.[5]

THREE TESTS OF CHARACTER

A leader's character generally is revealed three ways. Most leaders deal with tremendous ambiguity on a daily basis. What gyroscope guides them? What controls or "brakes" does the candidate possess to rein in errant inclinations?

TEST # 1: DOES THE LEADER HAVE A STRONG MORAL/ETHICAL GUIDANCE SYSTEM THAT FUNCTIONS WELL IN AMBIGUOUS SITUATIONS?

As I researched the background information for the Frank Raines profile, I repeatedly asked myself, was he seeking to bring clarity to Fannie Mae's accounting practices, or was he using ambiguity to obscure what the financial giant had done? I honestly don't know, but it was hard to conclude that any effort to bring clarity prevailed.

Recently, a head of a West Coast entertainment company told me that his company's outside investment counsel approached him with an offer to give him access to special investment advice. Though not stated overtly, the investment advisor implied that if the leader retained the investment firm to manage the employee's 401(k) plan, he would be allowed to participate in "sweetheart deals," in which only insiders could invest. This leader wisely consulted with a few key board members who quickly advised against any continued association with the investment firm.

Most of us fail to see that we face tests of integrity in the work setting every day. We dwell in the "shadow lands," and the right decision may not be obvious in the dim light. Many choices presented to us in the shadow land are subtle, thus the right or wrong action is not immediately clear. These muted or even distorted choices appeal to some felt need, but often they are accompanied by an inner reservation that suggests this may not be a good choice. It just "seems wrong." Effective leaders learn to pay attention to and heed these subtle signals. Getting counsel from a trusted advisor often puts more light on the question.

TEST # 2: DOES THE LEADER MAKE DECISIONS JUST FOR EXPEDIENCY?

A few years ago I facilitated a leadership team development exercise for a large construction company in the mid-Atlantic region. On a break I sat down to organize my thoughts for the next part of the meeting and overheard a conversation between the CEO and one of his key lieutenants who were standing nearby. When the CEO asked his colleague about the "little asbestos problem" in the building he was renovating, the lieutenant said that they had decided the only way to finish the building on budget and on schedule was to "look the other way." Building codes would have required that the asbestos be eliminated—a time-consuming and expensive delay. There was no pushback from the CEO. Ironically, blazoned across all the company's marketing materials was the company's undying commitment to integrity.

Expediency by its very nature places performance over principle. Driven usually by self-interest, leaders who go for the expedient action rather than the right one show their overall lack of concern for others and a failure to observe even basic moral/ethical standards. An expedient act often compromises character.

TEST # 3: DOES THE LEADER HANDLE ADVERSITY WITH GRACE?

How we handle adversity tells a lot about us and our character. We can only look good for so long until adversity strips away our façade. Adversity pulls at our dark side and compromises our character.

Sometimes we feel like a tube of toothpaste. Tough times come along, and they squeeze out what's really inside us. We become more of who we already are. Enough pressure, and our flaws start to impact our decisions and our behavior toward others. When we see a leader's character flaws surface under duress, narcissism and bad judgment can result in stupendous suffering of stockholders, employees, and vendors, as well as in the loss of trust of an organization in general.

I have always liked Anthony Hopkins's line near the end of the movie *The Edge*, where he says, "We are all put to the test, but it never comes in the form or the point we would prefer, does it?"[6] I don't know anyone who plans their adversity—it is not something we control. Perhaps that's why adversity is good for character. Its apparent randomness purifies our perspectives and reminds us of our humanity—that our control is actually quite limited. Those who are trained by it are often better for it. Just as Hopkins becomes more resilient throughout the film, they are more resilient, better able to take on more difficult challenges and become more respectful of others.

STAYING ON TRACK IS AN EXERCISE OF CHARACTER

Among the thousands of leaders I've interviewed, some possess qualities that make their character deeply rooted. These qualities strengthen their inner gyroscope, they moderate any tendency to be expedient, and they mitigate the potentially crippling effects of adversity. These leaders possess a sense of calm, even temperedness, and steadiness. They tend to be steady under pressure. They seem to actually get stronger through adversity.

Those who lack these qualities tend to be tense, irritable, and moody, and they don't handle pressure well. They are overly sensitive and take criticism deeply and personally. They're often critical of others. These individuals are more fragile under stress. They are more emotionally volatile and tend to be suspicious of others' motives. They complain a lot, have trouble connecting with others, and lack empathy. They are less resilient.

At the end of the introductory chapter, "Derailed," I introduced four character-based qualities. As we saw in the six profiled leaders, the unmitigated expression of the dark side of these four character dimensions renders ineffective any person in leadership or in any other role. Table 1 shows the four qualities and the derailment behaviors associated with them.

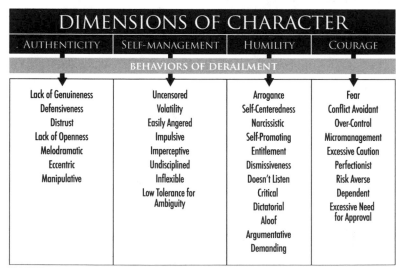

DIMENSIONS OF CHARACTER			
AUTHENTICITY	SELF-MANAGEMENT	HUMILITY	COURAGE
BEHAVIORS OF DERAILMENT			
Lack of Genuineness	Uncensored	Arrogance	Fear
Defensiveness	Volatility	Self-Centeredness	Conflict Avoidant
Distrust	Easily Angered	Narcissistic	Over-Control
Lack of Openness	Impulsive	Self-Promoting	Micromanagement
Melodramatic	Imperceptive	Entitlement	Excessive Caution
Eccentric	Undisciplined	Dismissiveness	Perfectionist
Manipulative	Inflexible	Doesn't Listen	Risk Averse
	Low Tolerance for Ambiguity	Critical	Dependent
		Dictatorial	Excessive Need for Approval
		Aloof	
		Argumentative	
		Demanding	

TABLE 1

The following four chapters show us how to stay on track by developing the critically important positive qualities that were absent in those who derail. We can derail-proof our work lives and grow our effectiveness as leaders by developing these four qualities. Their development holds the promise of giving us unassailable character, which is how we stay on track.

THE REAL DEAL

"False face must hide what the false heart doth know."
—MACBETH[1]

Several years ago, a friend invited me to a citywide "prayer breakfast." About five hundred business types gathered at a well-known Chicago hotel to hear an inspirational speaker. Toward the end of the meal, the emcee introduced the speaker and provided a few headlines of the phenomenal story we were about to hear from this Vietnam War Medal of Honor recipient.

Although in his fifties and somewhat nondescript, this former special forces veteran still looked to be in great shape and spoke with the confidence of a man who had survived great personal danger. On many occasions former Vietnam POW Sen. John McCain has detailed the deplorable treatment of U.S. POWs at the infamous "Hanoi Hilton." Our speaker's mission during the Vietnam War was to go behind enemy lines and to study the feasibility of a rescue of American POWs. His insertion into North Vietnam came through Russia. Secret operatives in the former Soviet Union were able to pass this war hero off as a Russian officer assigned to inspect the POW camps in and around Hanoi because of his language fluency and knowledge of the culture. With falsified documents he landed in Hanoi and began his inspections several days later, following North Vietnamese officials' approval of his "orders."

I've seen grown men cry, but not five hundred at once. Never before had I been so moved as our speaker detailed the treatment of American POWs. Unable to risk his cover, this man watched American POWs get beaten with stiff rods while their interrogators sought to extract "confessions" of their crimes against humanity. One man made the sign of the cross between each excruciating blow of the rods. At the end of what seemed like an hour of this inhumane treatment, the man bleeding profusely from his head and torso looked at his tormentors from the filthy floor of the interrogation room and forgave them for their mistreatment.

After witnessing this, the undercover soldier feigned illness to return to his quarters, where he wept uncontrollably. In a pool of his own tears he asked God to give him the faith that he had just witnessed. After detailing other POWs' heroism in the presence of unconscionable treatment, he described his daring escape orchestrated by Navy Seals at a prearranged rendezvous with an American fast-attack submarine in the South China Sea.

A thunderous and sustained standing ovation confirmed that each man in the audience had been transformed by this extraordinary story. We each thanked our table hosts profusely and left with inspired hearts.

Astoundingly, the veteran refused to accept the generous honorarium the breakfast organizers wanted to give him. He preferred instead to have the breakfast organizers give the money to a non-profit organization for the homeless. A particular inner-city mission served hundreds of destitute individuals each day and risked losing their occupancy permit due to some out-of-code fire doors in the kitchen. Many gave generously to this selfless request.

About two weeks later, my host for the breakfast called to say he had some bad news. In attempting to transfer the money, it had been discovered that our speaker was a fraud! His entire story was fabricated—nothing of what he described actually happened. Upon further investigation his entire story unraveled. He never even served in the army. He was a total psychopath, and we all had been duped!

IF YOU WORK THERE, THEN BE THERE

A failure of authenticity frequently contributes to derailment. It is not a blatant attempt to deceive, as in the example above, but at the heart of the problem is a failure to let others see who we really are. Not engaging with others in a meaningful way is always a tip-off.

Bob Nardelli's private elevator at Home Depot ensured that he didn't have to engage with most of the other employees. When a leader is not out in contact with the ordinary folks, it conveys the "Wizard of Oz Syndrome." There's some guy behind a screen who speaks with a loud, thunderous voice, trying to control our lives. We know he is just an ordinary person who is trying to appear as someone he's not.

In stark contrast I recently had breakfast with a Fortune 25 CEO at his company's cafeteria in the corporate headquarters building. As we rode the regular elevator, he spoke with several people on a first-name basis. He made a kind remark to the cashier in the employee cafeteria. He was genuine. This CEO wasn't trying to be someone he wasn't, and the members of the organization obviously respected him for it. He was extraordinarily competent at leading his company and achieving results, but he was also authentic.

Lack of engagement was one of Steven Heyer's most significant problems. He never really unpacked his emotional bags at Starwood. He didn't spend enough time at the headquarters engaging with the people who did the work of the organization. Individuals don't trust someone when they are not sure if the person is authentic and truly committed to the well-being of the organization and its employees.

We all know people who do not seem authentic, and we have likely worked for some of them. Their manner or their inconsistency in how they acted with different people makes us a bit queasy. Such people, when they are talented, rise rapidly in organizations. They have great individual careers, but their damaged relationships with their subordinates inevitably undermine their leadership.

EVERYONE WEARS A MASK

We all have masks that we use to interact with those around us. It's part of normal psychological functioning that helps us interact with others more smoothly. Masks give us the predictability, safety, and efficiency we need in our daily interface with others, and when we don't wear the right one, it jolts those around us and makes them uncomfortable.

Most people don't act the same in a job interview as they do when they're horsing around with their best friends. If they do, they are fired before they are hired. When a coworker asks, "How are you?" the prescribed response is to smile and say,

"Fine." Most of the time, the person asking doesn't actually want to know how the person is. And when we are the respondent, we are quick to respond, "Fine," even when we are absolutely miserable. It would be awkward to not follow these customs. If, in response to the question "How are you?" you said, "Well, I'm having an existential meltdown and rethinking the meaning of life," people will start to avoid you.

We also wear masks when we're just making small talk. This ranges from, "Could you believe the traffic this morning?" to "Did you watch the game last night?" We usually don't talk about deeper topics at parties or in the break room. We talk about our children, gas mileage, sports, movies, and the weather. We complain about taxes or the heat or how busy we are.

At work, the topics may be a bit more serious: "Did you hear that Sally is going to quit on Friday?" or "Have you heard there may be some layoffs next month?" but the discussion is still about "the news." Learning to talk easily about these kinds of "non–world peace" topics is part of being skilled socially.

We wear masks in formal settings, like a banquet, a wedding, or at work. When we wear the work mask, we are usually trying to get something done. We meet with our boss or the project team, and the tone gets more official. We use a very different vocabulary, like "strategic," "deliverable," "work product," "quality metrics," and so forth. Another dimension of the work mask includes "opinions." I've sat in hundreds of meetings where attendees give their opinions on whatever is being discussed. Much of the time I sense that the opinion being expressed has been weighed against what's expedient, politically safe, and not likely to offend the boss.

Masks make our interactions with others easier, but people who don't or can't get beyond the persona seem shallow or "fake." Deeper and far more profound aspects of who we are exist underneath these masks. Our beliefs and convictions reflect much more about who we really are and, when strongly held, drive us to act even at great personal risk.

THE REAL THING

When we see people who actually are who they "appear" to be, we call them authentic. There's an alignment between the inner person and the outer person . . . between their beliefs, values, and behavior. "Authenticity" most often refers to things, like documents or paintings, implying that these objects are genuine, not counterfeit. Our trust in and value of an object ties directly to its authenticity or genuineness.

We use this same word to describe people. We trust someone who is authentic and distrust someone who has a lack of genuineness. Actually, the Greek origin of *authenticity* means "acting on one's own authority—entitled to acceptance as factual."[2] It has been my observation that effective individuals frequently venture "self-authored" ideas, which reflect a person's true beliefs and convictions. I may disagree with their idea, but my respect and trust of the person rises when I feel I'm dealing with someone who is real, open, direct, trustworthy, and genuine.

Sometimes we hear someone described as an "empty suit." We wonder if that person has any real convictions. David Gergen wrote about how people feel about leaders who lack authenticity: "They are not sure they know exactly who is stand-

114

ing behind the public mask—some ask if he knows himself—and they become distrustful."[3]

James Kouzes and Barry Posner's research for their book *Credibility* determined that an executive's credibility is the cornerstone of effectiveness.[4] Our credibility results directly from our authenticity! It is the character dimension that affirms that we are a real person—what you see is what you get. We become credible when we are authentic. We are taken seriously. We are viewed as trustworthy.

Every manager should be able to answer these questions before taking over a department or a function or even the whole organization. Take off the mask and lay down the baseline of authenticity from which to build:

1. Who am I?

2. Where did I come from (personally and professionally)?

3. What are the values that fundamentally guide me?

4. Who has had a major influence in my management philosophy?

5. What experiences (positive and negative) in my background have prepared me for this role?

6. Why am I the right person for this position?

7. What are my expectations for the team?

For some, personal transparency feels like a loss of control. We just can't push through and break the authenticity barrier to express who we really are. But when we answer honestly these or similar questions, we are being authentic. It makes us more credible and trustworthy in the eyes of our colleagues.

LACK OF AUTHENTICITY

Jesuit priest John Powell posed a very important question in the title of his book *Why Am I Afraid to Tell You Who I Am?*[5] The book is about the answer to the question, but essentially the message is, "If I tell you who I really am and you reject me, that is all I have." Admittedly, becoming more authentic is not without risks; however, a person's unwillingness to risk expression of their true beliefs and convictions and to break through the "authenticity barrier" eventually becomes their undoing. Lack of authenticity becomes a derailment factor.

Lack of authenticity takes any number of forms. We see it when a person gets defensive and we ask ourselves, "What belief or conviction is that person guarding?" When a person displays a lack of openness, our trust diminishes. We are particularly distrustful of the leader whose mask is always on—she never seems real. We question whether or not we are being deceived. Being authentic makes a leader more trustworthy.

I occasionally talk with managers who are preparing to speak to their employees. A manager who gets defensive doing Q&A with an employee group loses credibility. If he cannot answer a question, I recommend he say, "That's a fair question, and it's perfectly okay to ask about that topic. I hope you'll understand that answering that question before all the facts are known could be misleading. I want to be respectful of everyone impacted by this decision. I need more time before answering that question, but I'll get back to you." Most employees understand and accept that kind of genuine handling of a question.

SAVE YOUR DRAMA FOR YOUR MAMA

Some of my most difficult consulting assignments over the years occurred in organizations that were highly emotional. We will talk more about emotional volatility later, but in some instances, excessive or exaggerated emotions hide a person's authentic self. For example, I worked with an individual whose frequent bluster hid his actual deep insecurity. I've actually described some companies as a "soap opera," and that may have been a disservice to *Days of Our Lives*. Any number of things in a workplace may provoke strong feelings, but when we begin to act like Scarlett O'Hara, our authenticity and credibility plummet. If you are a leader or aspire to be one, check the melodrama at the door.

Also, if you spend all your time in your garage trying to invent fusion, you can afford to be as weird as you want. If you're going to work in an organization in which collaboration with others is essential, being the company eccentric doesn't play well. Smiling, asking about other people's kids, and railing about who was just voted off *American Idol* is what most normal people do. It's okay to be brilliant and to be engineering the next patentable medical device, but also learn to connect with regular people. Being eccentric can derail you in a hurry.

BECOMING AUTHENTIC

Here are some important aspects of being authentic that you can work on:

1. Get comfortable in your own skin—find out what you like about yourself.

2. Never, ever be arrogant.

3. Tell the truth.

4. Treat others with respect.

5. Build rapport with others by asking them questions about themselves, then listen attentively.

6. Use self-deprecating humor. It personalizes you to others and makes you real.

7. Share your true beliefs and convictions with those you trust.

STAYING ON TRACK

Lack of authenticity in any form has a high probability of derailing a career. Our credibility depends on developing and expressing clear beliefs and convictions.

Sometimes it's too late. Southern gothic writer Flannery O'Connor wrote the very disturbing short story "A Good Man Is Hard to Find." While considered one of the greatest short stories ever written, the ending of the story is deeply troubling. A family headed to Florida on vacation has a minor auto accident and is discovered on a remote road by a group of escaped prisoners. Each member of the family is murdered, but the narcissistic grandmother, the main character of the story, babbles insipidly, trying to flatter "The Misfit" to get him to spare her life. When the grandmother realizes her life is about to end, she finally becomes real, perhaps for the first time in her empty life.

At her core she's actually a caring, compassionate, and authentic person, but it takes this desperate circumstance for anything genuine to emerge. Just after he shoots her, The Misfit says to his companions, "She would have been a good woman . . . if it had been somebody there to shoot her every minute of her life."[6]

A wise friend of mine used to say, "Everybody ought to get fired once." It's true that some may need a harsher wake-up call to get to the core of who they really are, but hopefully for us it's more like the prodding of a mentor versus our derailment.

GET AHOLD OF YOURSELF!

"The bridge washed out and I can't swim and my baby's on the other side."[1]

—WARNER MACK
country songwriter and singer

The late-afternoon sun dances on the blue-gray waves of the Atlantic. A mile or so across the channel, Caribbean music drifts faintly over the water while camera-laden Spring Break tourists board a Disney cruise boat. Gradually the ominous outline of the dark hull appears on the horizon, three-fourths of its 360-foot length hidden under water. A few other men and I watch quietly from a different dock—no cameras or piña coladas allowed here. Thus began a three-day "Tiger Cruise" at five hundred feet under water, nestled between Mk-48 torpedoes and Tomahawk cruise missiles on a nuclear-powered fast-attack submarine.

The internal workings of a sub are an engineering marvel. Outfitted with the latest technology to accomplish its clandestine missions, the interior felt unexpectedly roomy, as I climb down the steel ladder. Flat-screen panels everywhere display critical, real-time navigational information. Parts of the boat—like the nuclear power plant, the sonar room, and the very secret communications center—were off-limits to us

visitors; other than that, we moved around with surprising freedom. We spent several days watching the crew practice maneu-
vers, such as "angles and dangles," steep turns while ascending
and descending. With our hands gripping something secure,
we held on as the boat performed a "rapid ascent," like the
fast-attack leaping above the surface in *The Hunt for Red
October.*

While the boat's technology, engineering, and weaponry
were amazing, the competence of the crew was even more
impressive. Many in their twenties, these young men epito-
mized professionalism and teamwork, demonstrating technical
mastery and disciplined attention to detail. What was truly
amazing, however, was the "social" mastery—their ability to
manage their work relationships with confidence and respect.
While any military organization operates a rigid authority
structure of rank and title, the atmosphere on the boat seemed
collegial. Leadership transferred from one man to the next
effortlessly. Mastery trumped rank. Highly knowledgeable and
experienced enlisted men trained young officers, respectfully
yet firmly. A senior chief diplomatically took a young officer off
to the side for a quiet conversation at the end of which I was
quite certain the ensign would never again repeat that proce-
dural mistake. This team of young men who normally live in a
very dangerous world worked in concert out of commitment to
a common mission.

Not every member of the crew rose to this level. One mid-
level officer created resistance in others through his routine
interactions. He had a gift of provoking irritation and radiated
negativity. This man reminded me of the "Lil Abner" character,
Joe Btfsplk, who had a perpetually dark rain cloud over his

head—he just seemed gloomy and pessimistic. Other officers avoided this man, who seemed both imperceptive and inflexible—a bad combination. They clearly did not respect him, and he didn't "connect well" with them. His repeated efforts to relate or to be "cool" fell flat and prompted even more derision. I don't know how the navy makes promotion decisions, but in most businesses, he would be a train wreck in the making. The chief difference I observed between this individual and many other members of the crew was self-management.

SELF-MANAGEMENT—WHAT IS IT AND WHY IS IT IMPORTANT?

Self-management may be best defined as skill, insight, sensitivity, impulse control, optimism, and persistence applied in the particular environment in which we work and live. It cannot be overstated how critical self-management is to success at work and how detrimental its absence is. Those who derail often fail to self-manage effectively.

A self-management deficit may manifest itself in a variety of ways. When I see Bobby Knight interviewed on TV, the first thing I always remember is the chair incident. Despite his tremendous coaching record, Knight's throwing a chair onto the basketball floor in a fit of rage still defines him today. In a February 23, 1985, game against Purdue, Knight received a technical foul for protesting an official's call. In a highly publicized volatile act, he picked up a chair from the Indiana bench and tossed it onto the playing floor. We occasionally see a "Bobby Knight" in the corporate world.

After speaking at a meeting in a Caribbean resort attended

by a number of members of a Dallas-based energy company, my wife, Anne, and I stood in line with one of the company's senior officers and his wife as we went through customs before returning to the United States. One of the "self-employed" baggage handlers walked up to the four of us and said, "You take care of me, and I'll take care of you." It was unmistakably clear what this man wanted. For a small fee, he would ensure the safe transit of our bags to the airline baggage area. If you travel internationally, you'll find this is a common custom, one that a wise traveler will go along with. The executive, however, became incensed, and said in a condescending tone, "I'll not be bribed," and turned away in a huff.

I didn't like it, either, but I felt that at least the baggage handler was telling us how the system worked at his airport. Sometimes wisdom says we have to accept the rules of a game, even though we might consider the rules distasteful. I did a quick mental calculation of what it would be worth to me to get my luggage on the plane and back home. Twenty bucks seemed like a small price to pay, and I slipped him the bill. Our luggage made it, but none of the senior executive's luggage was ever found, including a suitcase containing expensive jewelry. Coincidentally, the board fired this executive a year later. One of the stated reasons was his lack of composure—he was too blustery and too easily angered.

Self-management helps us regulate what we do and also what we say. We have likely benefited from a "word fitly spoken," as the Old Testament author of Proverbs expressed it. He suggested that well-spoken words have the value of gold apples in a silver basket! Words not fitly spoken just as easily alienate and create conflict.

EMOTIONAL INTELLIGIENCE: "THE SINE QUA NON OF LEADERSHIP"

In the last few decades, this "self-management" ability has been formally studied and written about extensively in the behavioral science world. Dr. Daniel Goleman states that in business, "IQ and technical skills are important, but 'emotional intelligence' is the sine qua non of leadership."[2] Emotional intelligence (EQ) generally comprises the capability to be self-aware, self-managing, interpersonally effective, stress tolerant, and optimistic.

Goleman asserts that EQ counts for 80–90 percent of the factors that distinguish average from outstanding leaders. His research indicates that the higher a leader rises in an organization, the less important technical skills become and the more important EQ becomes.

In one study, self-management accounted for a 78 percent difference in profit contribution by partners in an accounting firm over those partners without those self-regulatory capabilities.[3] A common axiom states that IQ (Intelligence Quotient) gets you hired, while EQ gets you promoted.

Members of the elite submarine service are generally considered some of the best and brightest officers and enlisted men in the U.S. Navy. The admissions process and testing standards make it one of the most intellectually gifted and elite groups in the military. Operating a nuclear submarine clearly requires some serious brain cells. While the individuals on the subs have an undoubtedly high IQ, what I noticed to be just as important during my visit was their ability to manage themselves, to "get along," to be adaptable, and to manage stress in a very constrained environment.

Another critical aspect of self-management is psychological stamina. I saw one lieutenant work an eighteen-hour shift and finally go to his berth at midnight. An hour after settling into a deep sleep, he was called to the control room to serve as "Officer of the Deck" because the captain insisted his best young officer be in control of the boat as they neared the Eastern seaboard. At 6 a.m., he then became the officer in charge of bringing the boat into port, which took another five hours. I would have been catatonic and in a fetal position in one of the torpedo tubes by this point.

SELF-/OTHER-AWARENESS AND DERAILMENT

Effective self-management is heavily dependent upon good self- and other-awareness. A lack of self- and other-awareness is a common denominator among those who derail. The ability to manage ourselves and to manage our relationships is heavily dependent upon our perceptiveness of what's going on within us and with others. Self- and other-awareness employs the ability to discern our own thoughts and feelings as well as the thoughts and feelings of others. Those who derail seem to lack this ability to discern.

Self-aware individuals pay attention to their emotions without being ruled by them. They observe the responses of others and are able to adjust their behavior to make their interaction more effective. They understand how to build on their strengths and observe their limits. They use feedback as a corrective mechanism.

Self-aware leaders reflect often on how they are doing and

are more inclined to work in harmony with their values and priorities. Decisions are more thoughtful and well intentioned. Their direction is clear and founded on clear rationale. They draw this direction from the deep well of personal reflection. Those who derail tend to be unreflective, imperceptive, undisciplined, and impulsive.

A SELF-INFLICTED WOUND

Between self- and other-awareness and self-management, one critical quality intervenes—good judgment. Think of this as a sequence as described in figure 2 below:

SELF-/OTHER-AWARENESS ➡ JUDGMENT ➡ SELF-MANAGEMENT

FIGURE 2

Most derailments are self-inflicted and precipitated by poor judgment. At the root of all EQ problems, judgment looms large for all of us trying to accomplish something of substance with our lives. Essentially, judgment accomplishes three things for us.

First, it helps us solve complex problems. Judgment helps us integrate knowledge, experience, intuition, and input from others to solve problems resistant to solution. Your baby may be on the other side, but don't jump into a raging stream if you can't swim!

Second, judgment performs an important regulatory role in our lives. How often have we wished we hadn't said something in a meeting? We all wish we could reel back in things we've said impulsively. Judgment helps us check strong emotions at the door, rein in impulsive urges, and keep our composure under stress. It helps us to anticipate consequences and to take precautions to avoid unintended consequences. Judgment provides us with tolerance for ambiguity, which so often accompanies corporate life. It has a calming effect when we're faced with daunting, seemingly unsolvable problems.

A client organization acquired another company, and fairly soon after the purchase, the CEO of the parent company replaced the head of the new acquisition. I attended the meeting in which the new CEO of the subsidiary introduced himself to the senior management team and talked about his management philosophy. He explained how a particular organizational structure had worked well in some other companies he had led and how he felt it should be considered for this company. In a breathtaking display of candor, one of the senior managers told the new CEO that he was wrong and that the structure he proposed would not work. As others in the room fidgeted uncomfortably, the CEO listened but frowned. This outspoken manager was gone within two months.

Speaking our true beliefs and convictions authentically often leads to credibility and trust. It also takes courage to speak "truth to power"—to tell the CEO or someone high up in the organization what you really believe—but personal directness must be tempered with good judgment. Good judgment on the part of the manager in the story above would have dictated that he exercise some restraint in the meeting and better understand the CEO's new structure and why he thought it was potentially relevant to their company before critiquing it. Good judgment would have also dictated that he take up his issues in private versus confronting the new CEO at the very first meeting of the management team. There is a time and place for speaking one's mind, regardless of the risks entailed, but this wasn't one of them.

Judgment performs another regulatory role in our relationships. For example, my grandma Goldie used to tell me, "Don't get your honey where you get your money." I know that workplace romances are common, and occasionally they work out. But most don't and often these workplace dalliances create pain and hardship for many people.

Carelessness in this area often has consequences. I don't know what Steven Heyer's "suggestive and provocative" e-mails and text messages said, but they got the attention of Starwood's board and ABC News. The inappropriate physical encounter with a female employee outside a restaurant restroom was also cited.

Homer's great mythic epic about Odysseus' journey in the ancient world included a memorable tale about the beautiful Sirens who lured travelers to their deaths even from great distances. Odysseus wants to see the Sirens but has himself lashed to the mast, so that he will not succumb to their seduction. It's been said that Jack Welch, the legendary chairman and CEO of General Electric, derailed *after* he left GE. His highly publicized affair with an editor/writer of *Harvard Business Review* tarnished his great legacy. Judgment lashes us to the mast so that we make good decisions about relationships. It's always easier to prevent a problem than solve a problem—good judgment fuels prevention.

Third, judgment makes us more discerning in our decisions. One day a pediatrician in our community called and asked to meet with me. As I listened to his story, an amazing narrative unfolded. This gifted physician went into pediatrics because he didn't get accepted to the orthopedic residency he preferred.

After being in a pediatric practice for ten years, he finally had the courage to admit that he didn't like working with children all day long. To alleviate the stress of working with patients he didn't enjoy, he bought a mountain house to visit on weekends. After a few years of making the long drive to the mountains, he bought an airplane so that he could get there more quickly. At this point he was in debt up to his eyeballs—the only solution was to take on more patients to fund his stress relievers! By the time he spoke with me, this doctor was in despair. Discernment makes us perceptive so that we're able to cut through the haze and see ourselves, others, and situations more clearly.

MANY DERAILMENTS CAN BE PREVENTED

The self-regulatory capability I'm describing guides us to a purposeful, thoughtful, and intentional existence both personally and professionally. Many of the things we regret in our jobs and our lives happened very impulsively. Impulsivity omits the judgment step shown in figure 2.

Both of my sons played Little League baseball. One chilly spring evening, Anne and I sat with other parents watching an important playoff game. Because it was dark at six thirty, field lights illuminated the ballpark. A nearby parent complained that he hadn't been able to get a hot dog that night because the hot-dog machine had blown a circuit breaker. One of the industrious "take charge"–type dads said, "Well, I'll fix that." He stormed into the snack shop behind home plate, opened the gray steel door of the circuit panel, and began flipping breaker switches. All of a sudden, the field lights went dark. The next thing we knew, "Mr. Electrician" sheepishly came back to his seat.

Our stadium used some kind of environmentally correct bulbs that required a twenty-five-minute warm-up period before they could be turned on. We survived the fallout from an unwise, impulsive move, but a lot of families had late dinners, grumpy kids, and homework not completed for the next day from the late-night finish of the game.

DEVELOP SELF-MANAGEMENT

There is some really good news about this topic. Self- and other-awareness, judgment, and self-management can be developed. Routinely, I see people develop these qualities and become more effective at relating to others, monitoring themselves, and controlling errant emotions. James J. Lindemann, president and CEO of Emerson Motor Company, pointed out, "Derailment factors are remediable, but an individual must be wired to do so."[4]

To get better at self-management, here is some wiring that I've found helps:

1. Grow in self-awareness by proactively seeking feedback from multiple sources.

2. Find a wise and trusted advisor to help you interpret various work experiences and what you hear from others.

3. Be receptive to information about areas in which you are less than stellar.

4. Fine-tune your ability to connect with others—smiling, eye contact, attentiveness, asking good questions.

5. Work on empathy—focus on what others are telling you about their priorities and needs.

6. Conduct a 360-degree feedback exercise. Talk to your human resources representative about how to participate in this powerful feedback process.

7. Identify the circumstances under which you are likely to lose your composure—develop the early warning systems described earlier. Be diligent to anticipate and "get grounded" before you enter potentially problematic situations.

8. Wait longer to say something in meetings—write it down and test it for appropriateness before you say it.

While a spontaneous decision to live large like the characters in *Thelma and Louise* has some appeal after a tough week, self-management says to save it for the movies. Many derailments reflect a dearth of self-management. Imperceptiveness, impulsivity, and lack of judgment and discernment usually pay painful dividends.

THE STAR OF YOUR OWN SHOW

"If somebody takes himself overly seriously in this company, they're going to have a long day. And they're probably going to have a shortened career."[1]

—JACK WELCH

My friend, Gene, is a professional touring and studio singer and musician in Nashville. He's a lead singer in his own right, but, as a background vocalist ("bgv" as they say in the trade), he works with the best—Tim McGraw, Faith Hill, Amy Grant, Vince Gill, Peter Cetera, and many other stars. Much of the time he's on tour with someone like Donna Summer or in the studio making a new recording destined to go platinum.

Occasionally he gets a call from a record producer requesting that Gene assist with a "custom project." A few years ago a familiar voice on the phone said, "Gene, I've got a carpenter from Wyoming who wants to be the next Garth Brooks. He brought his guitar and his life savings to town to cut a CD. Could you spare two days in the studio to back him up?" Gene had a seam in his jammed schedule and agreed to help out the carpenter, one of countless aspiring musicians with big dreams.

We see them every year on *American Idol*—big dream, no talent. The carpenter didn't have timing, pitch, pocket, or feel. He just lacked musicality. With computer technology you can apparently make just about anybody sound passable, but it was going to take a lot of technology for this nail driver to become a singer.

The first day in the studio didn't go well. Gene is the consummate professional musician. He works with the best, so when he heard the carpenter from Wyoming, it was easy for him to be judgmental. "This guy's wasting his time and money . . . he's chasing the wrong dream." Gene's heart just wasn't in it. It was hard for Gene to ignore his musical training and standards of excellence.

It takes about five minutes to learn that Gene oozes character and integrity. On his drive home that afternoon, he had a talk with himself and realized he had the sorriest attitude south of Wichita. "I'm not God. Who am I to judge whether he's chasing the wrong dream?"

He knew that he had brought a different work ethic to the studio than if Faith Hill had been there. He vowed to bring his A-game the next day. "I've got to do the best I can do to help that carpenter be successful. It's my job to serve him and to bring out the very best music that's in him. I'm not going to be frustrated by his lack of musicality . . . My job is to do everything I can to help him realize his dream."

The next day, Gene brought a transformed heart to the studio. The whole atmosphere in the studio changed. The carpenter seemed to be more relaxed, and the recording session went much better. Was Gene watching the birth of a star? Likely not, but there was a redemptive quality in the room—humility.

Gene once told me that we are all constantly looking for ways to exalt ourselves. He said that when we're willing to shrink ourselves, the whole world gets bigger. No doubt, that Wyoming carpenter's world became a lot bigger that day.

WHAT IS HUMILITY IN THE WORKPLACE?

In a prophetic 2005 *Wall Street Journal* op-ed piece, former chairman of the Securities and Exchange Commission Arthur Levitt Jr. wrote:

> While the particulars of each of the recent CEO departures are unique, just about all post- Enron CEO firings involved talented, powerful individuals who conflated their positions with their personalities. Like modern-day sun kings, they thought the company was them; there was no distinction between the company and the CEO. . . . Gone are the days of the autocratic muscular CEO whose picture appeared on the covers of business magazines. . . . The imperial CEO is no more.[2]

Humility is not a quality we automatically associate with the workplace. Many of the people we think of in leadership roles have big egos and a high need for recognition. My first impulse is to think that humility belongs more in a religious context. We have an image of a self-effacing monk working tirelessly with the poor, then going home at night to have a meal of whole-wheat bread and home-grown vegetables with an early bedtime and no TV. My respect for individuals who work in selfless roles runs deep, but it's a very different world in which most of us spend

60 percent of our waking hours in our high-pressure jobs with managers who demand excellence.

Humility also seems a bit pedestrian as a topic and maybe even a bit boring for a business-oriented book. This is a subject that probably belongs in a coffee table book with dozens of inspirational sayings by someone we've never heard of super-imposed on beautiful images of tranquil waterfalls.

What place does humility have in the workplace, and what are the consequences of its absence? Author Jim Collins shocked the business world when his research surfaced that if you look at purely financial metrics, the most spectacularly successful lead-ers possess an odd combination of personal traits—extreme per-sonal humility and intense professional will.[3]

Collins further explained that these great leaders channel their ambition toward building their organization rather than personal aggrandizement. Individuals who knew the leaders described in Collins's research used words like "quiet, humble, modest, reserved, shy, gracious, mild-mannered, self-effacing, understated, did not believe their own clippings."[4] Leaders who had the most dramatic corporate performance possessed these qualities, along with a fanatical need to achieve results.

IT TAKES HUMILITY TO RECOGNIZE THE NEED FOR TEAMWORK

Conversely, the absence of humility often leads to derailment. Patrick Gelsinger, senior vice president of the Intel Corporation, indicated that "lack of humility is the big derailment issue."[5] Michael Volkema, chairman of the board and former chief execu-tive officer of Herman Miller, pointed out that lack of humility often manifests itself in the form of too much self-interest. Most work in the organization is done by teams, and he indicated that when someone takes excess credit, he will "get cut out from the herd pretty fast."[6]

Self-confident competence in our jobs and humility go hand-in-hand. During the last few weeks of my father's life, hospice came in to assist my mom with his care. I've worked with some of the most powerful and skilled leaders on the planet, but I don't think I've ever seen anyone as capable as these kind and gracious "caregiver leaders." The work they did was of the most humble nature imaginable, but they carried out their responsibilities with competence and confidence. They provided leadership, direction, and encouragement to my whole family during a difficult transition.

Humility is not about being self-deprecating or arrogant. It's about self-forgetfulness, remembering that in our jobs we're seeking to serve others. All jobs have a "That's why I'm here" factor. The "why" is usually to serve a customer or to provide information or resources to someone who serves a customer. Humility is about an accurate self-assessment—"My job is important, and I need to do it well"—but it's also the freedom to not inflate who you are or what you're doing.

When I speak to groups of CEOs, I often ask them a question: "Who do you think is more powerful . . . you or the people in your organization?" First, it's very quiet, followed by a ripple of nervous energy. Finally, a brave soul or two say, "The people."

Whether a CEO is willing to admit it, there is a tremendous interdependence between a leader and the members of the organization being led. A leader will not be successful without the alignment and support of those people doing the work of the organization. In a way, it's quite humbling, because it seems inconsistent with the power a CEO expects to wield. It's like the old axiom, "If the leader didn't come to work today, everything would probably still get done; if the people didn't come to work today, nothing would get done." The cartoon below captures this idea.

"While you were out, sir, the company, rudderless and adrift, operated pretty much the same as always."

Leaders with humility recognize that other roles in the company are also critical to its functioning. I participated in a succession planning discussion recently where it's anticipated that the CEO will retire soon. The conversation calmly acknowledged the expected smooth transition to the person presently being groomed for the role, who will likely take over by the end of the year.

Then, a bolt out of the air—one of the board members mentioned that Julie was also thinking of retiring at the end of the year . . . Julie being the CEO's executive assistant for the past twenty years. The room suddenly became quiet, and one board member actually said, "Oh my gosh! What are we going to do?" Julie had quietly and humbly served the CEO and the board for over twenty years. She was the institutional memory and had been at the epicenter of every important milestone in the company's life. Her quiet competence made her invaluable.

Humility at work also means we are coachable. "Coachability" has nothing to do with age or position. I've met with brash younger executives who you couldn't tell what time it was without some pushback. I worked with a CEO of a Fortune 500 company many years my senior who frequently had me stop by when I was in the home office of the company he led. His depth of background and experience made him a highly regarded leader in his company and in his industry. During our visits, he always requested advice about his leadership. Trust me, this man had forgotten more about leadership than I knew, but he was still a learner. His humility gave him an unquenchable thirst for learning and insight, and he sought to learn from anyone he could.

I'm often surprised at how hard people fight for titles in organizations. A title is probably best viewed as a means to quickly convey to outsiders what my job is. In many companies where I work, titles become the foundation of people's self-esteem. As author Stephen Covey points out, those with the biggest titles at the top of truly great organizations are "the most humble, the most reverent, the most open, the most teachable, the most respectful and the most caring."[7]

HOW THE ABSENCE OF HUMILITY
GETS US IN TROUBLE

In my research of the highly placed leaders I profiled earlier in the book, it became very apparent that arrogance was a key contributor to their derailments. If humility is having an accurate self-image and being other-oriented, then arrogance is its mirror opposite. Each executive profiled manifested this debilitating quality.

Arrogance is presumptuousness, overbearing pride, and an unwarranted, exalted sense of self-importance. Arthur Levitt Jr. wrote that today investor communities are looking for CEOs "who are more likely to fly under the radar, eschewing personal acclaim in favor of team-building and corporate success."[8] James Lindemann said that arrogance is most often seen in the form of self-promotion and entitlement. Most derailed executives believed "a particular job was owed to them."[9]

Lest we think that arrogance is a foible only in profit-driven business settings, it has nothing to do with the level at which we work in an organization or the nature of the work we do. As I mentioned earlier, some of the most humble individuals I know serve in nonprofit organizations, but there are others in religious or charitable groups who epitomize hubris and presumption.

WE'RE ALL SUSCEPTIBLE
TO ARROGANCE

Early in my career, a client requested I meet with a prospective merger partner in the financial services industry. The schedule was tight, so for a week I flew around in a private jet to various cities, and at each location I was whisked away to my meetings in a waiting planeside limo. I stayed in beautiful hotels and generally had a bevy of people making sure that every detail of my trip ran smoothly.

By the end of the week, I was getting used to being treated like I was important and drove home on Friday night a bit full of myself. Anne greeted me at the door with her normal cheerfulness and then dropped the bombshell on me: one of the toilets was clogged, and a plumber wanted a budget-busting amount of money for the repair. This was not the sort of clog that a plunger would take care of with a few well-aimed thrusts. A cloth diaper was lodged in a region of the toilet I didn't know existed and required a hands-on approach to solve. The sights, smells, and sensations were memorable. I didn't want to spend the money for a plumber, so after several hours of personal immersion in the project, the toilet finally cleared. I felt as though I needed to be taken to the nearest hazmat center and sprayed down from head to toe for exposure to germ warfare. I went to bed that night in a really foul mood.

The next morning I woke up laughing. Immersion in the toilet was actually a perfect way to end the week and bring me back down to reality. The toilet was real life, not flying around in a private corporate jet, staying in expensive hotels. We all need a good "in the toilet experience" every now and then to remind us who we really are.

One of the most revealing tests of a person's character is power. We see in the profiles of derailment that power, in many cases, became self-serving. The "trappings" of power often tell a lot about character. Bob Nardelli created a nine-car personal parking area for his cars underneath Home Depot's corporate office. His private elevator went from his personal parking area straight to his private office on the top floor of the building— no stopping for the little people! Contrast that with Wal-Mart's headquarters. Every person who visits the home office in Bentonville, Arkansas, comments on their very modest offices, including the CEO's.

Psychologists explain "overcompensation" as an attempt on a person's part to overcome a perceived inferiority. When I meet with executives who are self-promoting, dictatorial, demanding, and dismissive of others, I always wonder what makes them feel so weak and insecure. The more blustery and entitled they act, the weaker they must feel.

Arrogance also feeds a judgmental attitude. One of the things I like about working with someone who is humble is that they tend to not be judgmental. They may have the highest standards, but rarely do I feel judged or condemned by them for something I don't know or something I cannot do. Judgmental individuals are deeply afraid of being judged and found wanting. Their perceived insecurities make them so.

DEVELOPING HUMILITY

When I interviewed Mike Volkema, in connection with this book, I asked him how he spotted lack of humility early in a young executive's career. He said:

> They are really out for themselves and don't have the best interests of the group or organization in mind. So it shows up in little things. It's not as overt as self-promotion, but their unwillingness to sacrifice on behalf

of the team just demonstrates itself in a number of ways. The group quickly picks up on it and says this is all about you.[10]

Lack of humility can be lethal to our careers. The following list will help you consider how to develop this vital quality:

1. Have an honest conversation with yourself about your own attitudes toward others. Do you feel smarter, more capable, or, in general, superior?

2. Be aware of self-promotion. Very few tasks are accomplished by individuals. We're highly interdependent in the modern organization.

3. Develop an attitude of gratitude . . . make a practice of recognizing others for their accomplishments.

4. Become more open to others and convey an interest in their opinions. Listen to what they have to say.

5. Be aware of how you may be perceived as aloof or withdrawn.

6. Get familiar with any non-verbal signals that you may be sending to others. For example, when we blow through pursed lips and tilt our heads sideways while casting our eyes upward, it's a powerful and dismissive gesture. Watch yourself in the mirror.

7. Ask a trusted advisor who's seen you in meetings or other interactions how you come across.

8. Try to develop an inner calibration for when

self-confidence crosses over to arrogance. Pay
attention to those signals.

It is difficult to overstate the importance of the virtue of
humility. When I speak to MBA classes at business schools, I
often caution students about arrogance. Many of these very
bright, competent young men and women feel that their new-
found learning compels them to be strategically brilliant and full
of corporate wisdom when they complete their degrees and
begin their new jobs. Many will make huge contributions to
their respective organizations, but arrogance and dismissiveness
of those with less academic training will quickly mollify the
value they bring. Humble competence is the fast track to the
best executive suites.

AN AMAZING ORDINARY HERO

*"You may not know this but . . . there's things that gnaw
at a man worse than dyin'."*

—CHARLEY WAITE
Open Range

Dallas Tower, this is Delta 923 on final approach runway
one three right."[1]

TWR: "Delta 923, wind is one one zero at eight knots;
you're cleared to land runway one three right."

923: "Tower, Delta 923 has an abnormal gear
indication. Request a low pass to allow visual
inspection on right main landing gear. It's not
indicating down and locked."

TWR: "Roger Delta 923. Cleared for low approach
runway one three right. Upon reaching departure
end, fly heading two three zero, climb and
maintain three thousand feet."

923: "Roger, after low approach, heading two three
zero and climb to three thousand feet."

TWR: "Delta 923, visual inspection confirms that your
right main landing gear is *not* down and locked.
State your intentions."

923:   "Delta 923 requests radar vectors to a local area
       to work the problem."
TWR: "Roger Delta 923, fly heading three zero zero.
       Contact Dallas Departure Control, frequency
       124.3."

This terse exchange actually took place between my father, the Delta captain on flight 923 from New York to Dallas, and the Dallas airport tower in 1966. The Convair 880 four-engine jet carried eighty-eight passengers plus a crew of six on board. Captain Jim Irwin explained later that the flight crew frantically searched their training manual to find a solution but to no avail. More disturbing, the manual did not have an emergency procedure for how best to land this jet with a landing gear jammed in a retracted position. He radioed for help and spoke with Convair's engineering team in California—they, too, had no guidance, given that this problem had never before occurred with this particular aircraft.

After consulting with Delta management, a decision was made to divert Delta 923 to Carswell Air Force base because of their superior emergency response capabilities and extra-long runway. They also were able to put fire retardant foam over the entire runway very quickly. What no one needed to say was that given the seriousness of the problem and lack of guidance from any authority on how best to land this particular plane, the prospect of a fiery crash with numerous deaths and injuries was almost a certainty. There was unanimous agreement among Delta's management, Convair, and the Carswell tower—Captain Irwin was the final authority on how best to land the plane.

My dad decided first to circle the field and burn up as much fuel as possible. The big decision was whether to belly land or to land with the nose and left main landing gears down, allowing the plane to settle on the right engine pod underneath the wing. Each approach had major risks. Belly landings often cause big explosions. Landing on the right wing could cause the plane to spin wildly out of control, followed by a big explosion. Neither option appeared good. Ironically, what my father couldn't have known was that less than twenty-four hours later, a South American airline would experience the very same problem with the same model jet. There, the pilot elected to belly land, resulting in massive damage to the airplane and numerous casualties.

Dad elected to land with the nose and left main landing gears extended. He requested that Carswell place foam down one side of the runway where the engine pod would scrape, allowing him to use the dry side of the runway to slow the crippled airliner's speed before the wing began to drag on the concrete runway.

During final approach flight attendants on Delta flight 923 prepared the passengers for impact. They mentally rehearsed their emergency procedures for deploying the evacuation slides out the doorways to get as many passengers as possible out before smoke and fire swept through the cabin. Many passengers wept quietly and joined hands all over the cabin in somber unity, knowing that within seconds their lives could be over.

How does a leader prepare for this kind of gut-wrenching event? Several years ago I rummaged around an old trunk in my parents' attic and made an amazing discovery. I found a list in my dad's own handwriting that documented many of his thirty bombing missions when he piloted a B-24 Liberator over enemy targets in World War II. The list read like a military history text, with each entry telling its own story.

His squadron bombed strategic German industrial strong-holds, such as Rosenheim, Brenner Pass, and Lintz. Some of the entries included the names of friends lost—men whose own planes had gone down or exploded in midair in that day's battle.

On Christmas Day 1944 over Innsbruck, this twenty-two-year-old pilot thought for an instant that he'd lost his left arm when a large piece of shrapnel from an exploding flak shell burst through the windshield. Despite his wound, he piloted his plane back to their base in Italy and was later awarded the Purple Heart.

His list of missions drew attention to how his courage and calm spirit were forged in a furnace of adversity. It is amazing to think about how this young man, as did so many others in the "greatest generation," strapped on a parachute over and over again and risked it all in machines that at times were marginally airworthy to defeat the intentions of a cruel dictator. Jim Irwin's character, steadiness, and quiet courage inspired his crew to stay the course and to execute their many missions. Remarkably, not one airman under his command was lost in combat.

Many years later Delta 923 touched down on the long run-way at Carswell, and eventually the right wing dipped toward the foamed side of the runway. Witnesses said sparks flew for a thousand yards when the lower engine cowling scraped the con-crete runway, but Irwin's skillful throttle control and careful braking kept the malfunctioning aircraft perfectly centered on the runway.

When the jetliner finally stopped, passengers quietly and calmly followed his instructions and exited the listing aircraft down the emergency slides. A front-page above-the-fold article in the *Atlanta Journal* reported, "According to the passengers, Captain Irwin landed the plane so smoothly, the lack of the right gear was hardly noticeable."[2] Delta mechanics who repaired the plane said the damage was amazingly minor—only a few hundred dollars of sheet metal was required to repair the engine cowling. They also located the faulty locking pin that prevented the landing gear from lowering into position.

The crew and others around him said my dad reacted as though this were just another landing. Oddly, he later told me that he felt tremendously afraid during the whole ordeal of landing his malfunctioning plane.

My father thought of himself as a very ordinary man, just doing his job. Isn't this really what courageous people are—just ordinary people doing extraordinary things . . . people who feel compelled to act on behalf of others when there is often significant personal risk involved? Courage is not being unafraid. It's about choosing to do the right thing under difficult circumstances. Courageous individuals are people not caught up in their own importance or presuming that they're somehow more virtuous or impervious than others.

We are surprised when we hear how ordinary people have rescued someone who fell into the path of a subway or from some other potential disaster. Their typical explanation is, "Someone needed to do something. I was there and just did what I could." They usually appear embarrassed about all the fuss being made over their heroic status, while they're being interviewed on Fox News.

THE COURAGE OF OUR CONVICTIONS

In an earlier chapter we talked about the masks people often wear to facilitate normal day-to-day interactions with others. I also stated that it's critical to go beyond the masks to know our true beliefs and convictions. Courage emanates from our resolute beliefs and core convictions. It follows that when we are not grounded at some foundational level in our beliefs and convictions, we will not be courageous. Absent any real beliefs and convictions, and the courage that rests on them, we become tentative, or worse, expedient. We then want to just get along and line up with the prevailing opinion.

Convictions reflect what we are convinced is true *and* noble. The problem is that some convictions address topics that do not rise to the level of meaningful importance. People getting really worked up about which beer is better always strike me as a bit superficial. A courageous act only occurs when we are also convinced that something is true and truly important, rather than simply a preference.

Braveheart, *Henry V*, and *Open Range* are all great movies where lead characters must decide which is more precious—their own lives or the ideals that liberate others? In *Open Range*, one of the best recent westerns, the Kevin Costner character, Charley Waite, poses this existential dilemma in cowboy vernacular. "There's things that gnaw on a man worse than dyin'."[3] In Waite's case, it's justice.

Courage never exists in a vacuum. It results from our internalized beliefs and convictions about how our lives should best be directed toward some noble end. But we most likely have never faced the "Give me liberty or give me death" option in a real circumstance. Our daily lives tend to be much more focused on having a stable job, our families, our friends, lowering our handicap, sending our kids to college, hobbies, and our "stuff."

Socrates said, "The life which is unexamined is not worth living."[4] A deeper examination of our lives can often form the beliefs and convictions that push us toward making hard and sometimes risky decisions. It is careful consideration about what's really important in life and toward what ends we intend to invest our time, talent, and treasure that gives us the courage of our convictions to implement those hard and sacrificial decisions.

COURAGE AT WORK

Jobs with opportunities to perform heroic acts involving great physical risk are rare. In some occupations, like firefighting, dramatic rescues are more a part of the normal job, but most of us go to the office or make sales calls or manage a group of people tasked with a goal to achieve.

Still, courageous acts in the work setting occur far more often than we might think. I believe most people are capable of being courageous in a broader sense by making hard decisions, disagreeing with the boss, firing someone, giving a marginal employee a candid performance review, questioning someone's expense report, taking an unpopular stand, delivering bad news about the quarter's results, or thousands of other actions that require acting in the presence of fear, anxiety, or risk. Simply telling someone the truth can be a courageous act. Convictions give us the courage to venture a self-authored opinion and to have a thoughtful, well-founded set of ideas to offer even when those ideas go against a more widely held view or even the view of our manager. A courageous act, by its very nature, means that we are moving against the resistance of someone else's deeply held view or that we are acting in the face of considerable risk. Whistleblowers often lose their jobs.

One of my first clients was a business whose customers had very high standards for the service they received. The CEO frequently challenged his organization to exceed the customers' expectations and earn their trust through superior customer service. The CEO created a formal statement of the company's credo, and he made frequent reference to this set of guiding principles. He insisted that company employees demonstrate respect for their customers, fully expecting those customers to reciprocate in how they treated members of my client organization.

One customer accounted for 25 percent of this company's revenue, the loss of which would seriously jeopardize my client's profitability. This particular customer had many highly compensated salespeople with big egos. Over time, these salespeople became more and more demanding. They even bullied my client's staff to get what they wanted. My client called the CEO of the customer company and said, "We value your business, but we value our employees even more. The abrasive, demanding, and demeaning treatment of our employees must stop, or we will ask you to take your business somewhere else."

My client exhibited tremendous courage in making the call. The loss of the customer would have been devastating to the company's financial performance. Surprisingly, the CEO thanked him for the call and apologized for his organization's behavior. He promised to remedy the problem immediately and thanked my client for his candor. They also set up a problem resolution "council" that sought solutions to any ongoing business problems.

This story is an important illustration of how courage to do the right thing results from clarity about what we believe. My client put great thought into his company's credo. His convictions about honoring and preserving his employees gave him the courage to risk a major financial disaster. Speaking truth to power does not always achieve the result we want, but it does make a major statement about character.

It is never easy to demonstrate courage in our jobs, because the stakes are often high. Our jobs certainly provide our livelihood, but they also provide our identity. The prospect of losing our jobs represents a threat to our security and our self-esteem. Telling the truth is sometimes not welcomed in an organization. We need to examine ourselves to discover our true beliefs and convictions about our jobs and the values of the organizations we serve.

THE ABSENCE OF COURAGE

In 1626 Swedish king Gustavus Adolphus commissioned the building of one of the most powerful warships of its day, the *Vasa*, and ordered the launch of the ship on August 10, 1628. I'm not making this up—a few hundred yards into the channel, the ship encountered a slight breeze, rolled to its side, and sank, while a huge crowd of Swedish citizens gasped in shock from the shore. This glorious feat of marine architecture had insufficient ballast.[5]

That explanation covers the physics. Why the *Vasa* really sank was an absence of courage. Before the *Vasa* was launched, it failed a stability test with a number of knowledgeable observers present, including several senior naval officers.

King Gustav placed enormous pressure on shipbuilders and

153

other officials to launch the ship by July 25, 1628, and threatened, "If not, those responsible would be subject to His Majesty's disgrace."[6] The man in charge, Admiral Clas Fleming, knew the ship shouldn't be launched but wouldn't convey this bad news to a very irritable king.[7] He would not speak truth to power.

The absence of courage shows up in a variety of expected ways, but also in some less obvious ones. In the example of the *Vasa*, fear, conflict avoidance, and need for approval were the manifestations of lack of courage. Lack of courage shows up in many organizations as micromanagement, failure to empower others, risk aversion, overcontrol, and perfectionism.

Often I've spoken with leaders about creating cultures that foster courage in their organizations. Some organizations unwittingly have done just the opposite. Professor Martin Seligman performed one of the most memorable studies in psychological research, which he later called "learned helplessness."

Dogs that had been conditioned with an electric shock while restrained internalized the sense that they were "helpless." Even given the opportunity to escape the shock, these conditioned dogs would not jump over a low fence to escape a new shock. They learned to be helpless.[8]

Leaders create learned helplessness in their organizations in a variety of ways. For example, the "punishment" of truth tellers extinguishes truth telling in a hurry. Micromanagement and failure to empower make people feel helpless and incompetent. Employees begin to protect their jobs rather than setting big goals and trying to achieve them.

We have likely worked in organizations that couldn't handle the truth, and those organizations undoubtedly had a variety of ways to extinguish truth telling. We may have hard choices to make regarding whether we challenge the norms in an organizational culture of truth suppression.

DEVELOPING COURAGE

The absence of courage in our jobs can manifest itself in behaviors serious enough to derail us. The absence of courage makes us tentative. Tentativeness makes us conflict avoidant, over-controlling, and cautious. We experience an excessive need for approval. The cure is to develop the courage of our convictions. Here are some suggestions for how it can happen:

1. Keep a journal about your experiences at work. Who do you admire? What inner convictions seem to guide them? What do they do that strikes you as courageous?

2. What are your convictions and bedrock beliefs? How clear are they? How confident are you that they will provide the needed foundation for courageous choices in tough situations?

3. Think about the influences that most shape your convictions. If it's primarily *People* magazine or *Entertainment Tonight,* consider a few alternatives. Try reading *Undaunted Courage* by Stephen Ambrose, *John Adams* by David McCullough, or the story of Esther in the Bible.

4. When you have to deliver tough news, being courageous is critical. Also, be savvy. Think about the timing and shape the message for the recipient. A trusted advisor can help you with this.

5. When you take a stand, make sure you have your facts right. The facts often help separate the courageous from the foolhardy.

6. Managers hate it when they have to do our thinking for us. Be sure to have several possible remedies for a problem, along with a recommended solution.

7. Be courageous but also be prudent about not throwing others under the bus. Stick to the facts and be solution oriented when in conflict with coworkers.

8. Be willing to exercise the "nuclear option" as a last resort. Quitting in protest, going many levels up the food chain, and being a whistle-blower should always be considered. Going straight to these extreme solutions gives us no opportunity to escalate the gravity of our protest, so starting with a less extreme option is probably prudent. Simply knowing that we're willing to "go nuclear" may fortify us for the more measured approach.

Peter Drucker said, "People who don't take risks generally make about two big mistakes a year. People who do take risks generally make about two big mistakes a year."[9] When we look back on our lives, our hearts will be glad that we acted with courage. Although my father passed away several years ago, not a month goes by without someone remembering his heroic landing of a disabled airplane and saving all those people's lives. We will also want to be remembered, and courage is likely to be an important aspect of that memory.

ON TRACK FOR
THE LONG HAUL

DE-
RAILED

FIVE CRITICAL
LESSONS LEARNED

When Anne and I bought our first home, there was a hall-way connecting the family room to the kitchen and dining room that I felt was a total waste of space. The hallway was also quite dark. There were other ways to access the adjacent rooms, so I thought the hallway would make a nice large closet.

Anne had a different vision. She wanted to transform the hallway into an art gallery. The only problem was that our "art collection" consisted of one unframed poster of a famous European castle left over from my bachelor days. In spite of this slight limitation, Anne insisted we go ahead and ask the electrician doing some other work in our home to hang art lights on a ceiling track to ready the space for our supposed future art collection.

Unbeknownst to me, Anne asked the electrician to hang *eight* art lights on the ceiling. When I threw the switch, there was enough wattage in that hallway to illuminate a major league ballpark.

I have a perfectionist streak that occasionally emerges, and I like walls in my house to be very smooth and straight. Now bathed in the brilliant luminescence of what must have been eight gigawatts of art lights, the truth of my new house's drywall emerged. The previously unnoticed curves, irregularities, small cracks, and heads of sheetrock nails all became visible in the intense light. This was going to require a lot of castle posters to cover the carnage.

The purpose of *Derailed* is to shed intense light on our vulnerabilities—the irregularities and small cracks and fissures that can cause us to derail, whether we are leaders, emerging leaders, or simply navigating a career. This chapter summarizes five critical lessons learned from the examples of derailed leaders earlier in the book and from the wisdom of others who have discovered the crucial principles for staying on track.

LESSON ONE—CHARACTER TRUMPS COMPETENCE

The six leaders profiled earlier in the book are all exceptionally competent. They are impressive in numerous respects, and all have track records of exceptional accomplishment. If we aspire to leadership, we should seek to be as smart, as disciplined, as focused on achieving difficult goals, as strategic, as insistent on the creation of processes that ensure quality, and as committed to finding great people to man our organization, department, or team as they were. Great leadership includes all these and many other qualities.

However, the glaring truth is that a leader is only as good as the character of the leader. While competence is absolutely essential, our character ultimately makes a greater impact on what we accomplish in our work and in our lives. Character as expressed in authenticity, wisdom, humility, and courage must ultimately form the substance of who we are if we want to have great impact.

During a week of daring space walks, astronauts from the space shuttle recently performed a number of repairs to the Hubble telescope. Some of the most important repairs included replacing several gyroscopes that hold the telescope steady while aiming at distant stellar objects. These gyroscopes are foundational to the success of the Hubble, and without them, the telescope cannot perform its intended function.

We need to constantly monitor the effectiveness of that inner gyroscope called character. We may need a repair or replacement to ensure that our inner guidance system is working properly. At some point the derailed executives profiled in this book lost their way. Their inner gyroscopes malfunctioned. Their failed character negated their extraordinary competence. We need to be competent *and* to have unassailable character.

LESSON TWO—ARROGANCE IS THE MOTHER OF ALL DERAILERS

While a failure of character can manifest itself in many ways, the most foundational and most self-destructive is arrogance. Just as humility seems to be at the epicenter of leadership effectiveness, arrogance is commonly at the root of a leader's undoing . . . and ours. The specific derailers that rendered the profiled leaders incapable of continuing in their positions varied, but there is an underlayment of arrogance in every one of their derailments.

Arrogance takes many forms. The most rudimentary is the self-centered focus that fosters a belief that I am central to the viability of the organization, the department, or the team. The resulting dismissiveness of others' contributions is inevitable.

When arrogance blossoms into hubris, a sense of entitlement results. "This place can't function without me, and I deserve special perks." I've seen this attitude in CEOs of huge companies, and I've seen it in secretaries of mom-and-pop companies. It's not a function of the size of the organization or the level of the person in that organization.

Aloofness, being critical, self-promotion, and not listening to others all tie to arrogance. Even when our achievements are modest, arrogance can exist. We need to be ruthlessly intolerant of this toxic character compromiser when we see it in ourselves.

LESSON THREE—LACK OF SELF-/OTHER-AWARENESS IS A COMMON DENOMINATOR OF ALL DERAILMENTS

Recently I was asked to facilitate a meeting for a board of an organization that imports furniture for the retail market in the United States. The fundamental purpose of the meeting was to help the board and the CEO get along better. There was a healthy exchange as the board and the CEO sought to clarify expectations of their respective roles. The meeting went quite well, until the board requested the CEO pay greater attention to the government trade representatives who heavily influence their ability to import their product without onerous tariffs.

Previously, the CEO had been in several "smackdowns" with a couple of the representatives and had nothing but derisive comments about them. A comment or two of acknowledgment by the CEO would have been perfectly acceptable and probably even consistent with how most of the board members felt. Something like, "I find some of the trade representatives very difficult to work with, but I agree with you on the vital importance of cultivating good relationships with them. I will redouble my efforts to reach out to them." The board would have been ecstatic to hear this.

The problem was that the CEO's dismissive rant kept going . . . and going . . . and going. The Energizer Bunny would have run out of power before his tirade was done. I watched the faces of the board members as they listened . . . initially surprise, then disappointment, then irritation. The meeting became the failure of a great success. The CEO just didn't get it.

As of this writing, I rate the CEO's chances of job survival on the low side of fifty-fifty. Why? He lacks self-awareness. When we feel very strongly about something, it's important to keep that in mind. Our convictions can overpower our judgment. Self-awareness would have guided this errant CEO in two significant ways.

First, he should have paid attention to how strongly he felt and reined in his feelings and his uncensored expression of those feelings. In reality, he may feel the representatives are lower than pond scum, but those feelings had no place being verbalized in the meeting.

Second, he should have monitored the faces of others in the room, which were brimming over with valuable feedback for him. The warning signals were all there. He had plenty of opportunity to heed them, but he didn't. The goodwill with the board created earlier in the day now evaporated.

To stay on track, we have to be effective at monitoring our

inner state . . . our thoughts, our feelings, our convictions. There may be a time to courageously fall on our sword, but it's usually not the time when most people do it. Lack of self-awareness, too little or too late, is the common denominator of all derailments.

LESSON FOUR—WE ARE ALWAYS WHO WE ARE . . . ESPECIALLY UNDER STRESS

For a number of years a major brokerage house screened its candidates for sales positions using an assessment center. The purpose of the assessment center was to simulate the typical daily activities of a broker and to test the candidate reactions to the type of stressful conditions commonly encountered on the job. Across the half-daylong event, the stress level grows as the candidates are subjected to increased demands to multitask. About mid-morning one job candidate exceeded his threshold of stress tolerance when dealing with a reluctant buyer on the phone. He finally screamed, "Just remember, no guts, no glory," slammed down the phone, and stormed out of the room. He was not hired.

Most people can look good for a thirty-minute interview, which is why many employment interviews are not particularly effective in surfacing who the person really is. We are always going to be who we are, particularly when stress is the precipitant to reveal what's inside. When we aspire to a life of substance as an emerging leader or in any career we pursue, we have to grow from the inside out. If we are shallow inside, we will get to the end of who we are very quickly. If we are substantive inside, we are more likely to endure.

Many people are "shallow copers." They're easily thrown off track, and that's why so few do work of any great significance.

I remember the day late in my sophomore year in college when I decided that I wanted my life to count for something significant. The change was dramatic. My grades shot up. What I read and how I thought about it were different. The people I spent time with changed. My aspirations grew. I decided that if I ever achieved financial gain, it would be great, but that money or status would not be the purpose of my life and work.

Whether we have an epiphany or not, there will likely be a moment when we can choose substance over style, character over charisma, and wisdom over want. These choices set in motion a very different approach to life and work. When we set our faces in the direction of significance, we begin to be transformed from the inside out. If we will always be who we are, it pays to consider deeply who we want to become and to make choices consistent with that intention.

LESSON FIVE—DERAILMENT IS NOT INEVITABLE, BUT WITHOUT ATTENTION TO DEVELOPMENT, IT IS PROBABLE

One beautiful, warm July morning a few years ago, a good friend and I went fly-fishing in a remote mountainous area of North Carolina. Because the location was unfamiliar and particularly rugged, we hired a local guide to take us to the headwaters of a well-known stream. The mile-and-a-half hike into the stream was arduous, particularly walking over the rough terrain in waders and carrying our gear. The guide encouraged us to stay the course and said, "The fishing is great, because no one else is dumb enough to hike in this far!"

After fishing for a while, we sat down on some boulders to eat lunch. A few minutes later, one of those brief but intense summer thunderstorms rolled across the mountains. The air temperature was in the seventies, but the rain was unbelievably cold, and the lush canopy blocked all but a few wispy rays of sunlight. In the suddenly chilly air, my fishing buddy and I slipped on the jackets we brought along in our gear bags.

A few minutes later I looked across at our guide. He wasn't talking and had a funny bluish cast on his skin. He then started shaking uncontrollably and could not make eye contact. While I'd read about hypothermia, I'd never seen anyone suffer from it or thought about how someone's core body temperature could drop so quickly even in the middle of summer. Some people with hypothermia die. Fortunately our guide did not.

Derailment may appear to occur precipitously, but in fact it's usually the consequence of many actions over time. Derailment is especially rooted in the failure to prepare, to grow personally and professionally, and to develop the qualities needed to stay on track. Our fishing guide experienced hypothermia because he didn't prepare—he failed to bring a jacket, a very simple but profound remedy for the extreme and unexpected conditions. He was very competent as a fishing guide. He knew how to expertly cast a fly rod and which flies to use on that stream, but he could have easily been a casualty of his failure to prepare.

Derailment is not inevitable, but without development, it is probable. Attention to our development means we must be constantly alert and self-aware and have a lifelong commitment to learn, to grow, and to prepare. It's also a recognition that, just as the mighty can fall, so can we at any stage of our career. One CEO with whom I spoke stressed the critical importance of dealing with potential derailment factors early in our careers while there is time to recover. "Once someone is in an organization too long, it's almost too late for them."

HABITS OF THE HEART
TO STAY ON TRACK

"It's hell to work for a nervous boss, especially when you're the one making him nervous."[1]

—WILLIAM ONCKEN

No parent ever wants to get that phone call. Ours came on a blustery night in late March after Anne and I arrived home from a concert. Anne checked the voice mail and suddenly went pale. At the same instant my cell phone rang, and our son's first words were, "Dad, I'm okay." He didn't sound okay, and he wasn't.

That afternoon, on the last run of the last day while snowboarding in Colorado, he went off a jump, caught way too much air, rotated, and landed on his back. His friend, a veteran snowboarder who watched the accident, screamed at him to not move. Within minutes the ski patrol painstakingly strapped him to a rigid board, gingerly loaded him into a red metal sled, wrapped him in heavy blankets, and took him down the snow-covered mountain to a waiting ambulance.

The orthopedic surgeon in Vail confirmed that his T11 vertebra exploded in the twelve-foot plummet—his back was broken. At this juncture, all our thoughts were catastrophic: Was his life as he knew it over? Would he be paralyzed? Would he even be able to finish college and graduate from the U.S. Naval Academy? Was his intended career as a U.S. Naval officer not to be realized?

This trauma for our family set in motion a mind-numbing array of decisions and logistics through the long and dreary night. The Sheppard Spinal Center, a world-renowned hospital for spinal injuries, flew our son to Atlanta on a specially equipped emergency air ambulance. A spinal surgeon at the center examined him at 3 a.m. and confirmed that emergency surgery would be required the following morning, followed by months of rehabilitation. The doctor's prognosis was guarded, but he expressed his intention to use a highly regarded new high-tech fusion procedure to repair the damage.

My most vivid memory during the whole ordeal was the perky and petite physical therapist who might have been five feet tall in high heels persuading our six-foot-two middle linebacker son to get out of his ICU bed and begin therapy the morning after surgery. The battle of the titans came to mind as he fought to stay immobile to avoid the horrific pain of compressing his now titanium-rod–reinforced, fused spine. After twenty minutes of polite cajoling, the therapist would not be denied. She put her face close to his and said quietly but firmly, "You may not think you're going to get out of bed this morning and walk, but you are, and it's going to be *now*!" The "now" part of the message contained an unmistakable tone of "do not trifle with me any further." Within a few minutes, he was walking up and down stairs. By God's grace he had sustained no damage to his spinal cord in the accident and eventually made a full recovery.

"CAN I SEE YOU IN MY OFFICE?"

There's also a call that we never want to get at work. It's the call where our manager says, with an unsettling tone, that he wants to talk to us. You know the company is struggling, or maybe you've had a sense that your job is on the bubble. Our work resides at the core of our self-esteem. We may say we're okay, but when our jobs are threatened, we get that sick feeling in our gut that says we are not.

The euphemistic message varies—"You're not the best fit with the requirements of the job," or "We're eliminating your position," or "We're downsizing"—but the meaning is unmistakable. In his inimitable style Ted Turner put it succinctly: "You're toast."

In difficult times, some organizations fail calamitously and the whole company shuts down—it goes out of business. A much more likely scenario is that companies use recessions to manage marginal or poor performers out of the organization. I've consulted with businesses during three significant recessions, and companies typically do not downsize their A-players!

Whether in good times or bad, why do people get fired from their jobs? Thomas R. Watjen, president and chief executive officer of the Unum Group, said, "People do not derail for technical reasons." He went on to say that when a leader derails, it's because of their inability to get people to work together effectively.

Watjen's views are consistent with other experts who point out that the overwhelming number of people who get fired have the necessary technical skills to do their jobs. What they lack are self-management and interpersonal skills. Watjen pointed out that getting people to work together becomes even more important at higher levels in the organization.[2]

Patrick P. Gelsinger works with one of the most recognized global brands for technology, but he also stressed the critical necessity of effective interpersonal relationships in getting work done in Intel's highly technically oriented organization.[3] An engine, no matter how simple or complex, must have oil to run smoothly. Good interpersonal relationships are the oil of any corporate machine.

People get fired even when they are strong contributors to their organization. Michael A. Volkema said, "Derailment factors can be fatal when they overwhelm a person's strengths."[4]

A generally accepted truism reminds us that prevention is the most elegant solution to a problem. What do we need to do to stay on track in our careers? How do we become one of the members that the organization considers essential even during difficult times? In essence, how do we prevent derailment? This chapter deals with five foundational habits for how we stay on track—how we *avoid* getting that dreaded call.

FIVE CRITICAL HABITS OF THE HEART

Habits are essentially patterns of behavior that, once established, are prone to continue. We all have them. Some habits are easy to form and are acquired with little thought, like eating ice cream. Habits that don't have an immediate or obvious payoff are more difficult. They are generally challenging to establish and must be intentionally formed. Personal discipline requires that we do certain things because we believe in their eventual value, like physical exercise.

The five habits we look at here are more the personal discipline kind. They require intentional and focused effort to habituate—to make a part of our established behavior—but the payoff is enormous. We stay on track!

THE HABIT OF OPENNESS

My dad served as a commercial airline pilot for almost forty years. The last ten years of his career, he flew from Atlanta to a number of major hubs in Europe. Navigation satellites guided the onboard computer to the correct destination. My dad commented one time that properly programmed in Atlanta, the computerized autopilot could actually fly the plane from Atlanta to the right country, the right city, the right airport, and then land the plane unassisted on the right runway. Eerily, in the middle of the night, on its own, the wheel would turn and bank the plane for a few seconds, as if a ghost were flying the plane. The ghost was really the autopilot correcting the heading when the jet stream blew the plane off course. The "navsats" provided constant feedback about the location of the plane and its heading.

The first antidote to derailment is openness to feedback. Feedback has the potential to keep us on course in our careers. Feedback from a wise and trusted advisor can be more valuable than gold, but it requires openness on the part of the recipient. The senior leaders I consulted about staying on track felt particularly strongly about this topic. Why didn't Carly Fiorina listen to her board and act on their recommendations? Leaders must follow their own compass while still being open and receptive to the wisdom of others.

People deflect negative feedback for a whole host of reasons, none of them good. Here are the top ten:

10. My job forces me to act in strange ways; I'm really not like that.

9. This timing was bad for my boss to give me feedback.

8. My boss knows my strengths but is totally offtrack about my weaknesses.

7. My boss really has it in for me.

6. I was that way at one time, but I'm a different person now.

5. Nobody understands the demands of my job.

4. My boss must have me confused with someone else.

3. My boss doesn't have a clue what my job is.

2. Everyone is just envious of my skills.

1. I really don't give a rip what my boss thinks.[5]

When we're in a work setting, we need to check our defensiveness at the door. Please note that I'm not talking about working in an abusive atmosphere in which we might be harassed, demeaned, or threatened. Rather, we need to be constantly tuned into the "satellites" around us that provide information about how we're doing. Just because our boss may be clumsy at giving feedback doesn't mean the feedback is not valid.

One corporate leader with whom I spoke used a visceral word to describe the importance of taking in information from trusted colleagues: "Make yourself *vulnerable* to feedback" [emphasis mine]. He went on to describe how feedback he received from his boss early in his career was so important, it fundamentally changed how he related to others. He learned the importance of respecting personal boundaries—for example, not calling coworkers at home about work-related matters except in the event of an emergency.

Openness to feedback reflects our interest in being a learning, growing person. Openness involves an active desire to know how I'm doing and an abiding intellectual curiosity about how to be better. Individuals who want to grow and develop learn to welcome feedback from others, particularly someone they respect. They're able to separate the wheat from the chaff—not all feedback is accurate or even useful. Growing individuals incorporate accurate and useful feedback to promote constructive change. One CEO with whom I spoke pointed out a particularly important caveat about the advice we take: "Don't get coached out of your strength." Sometimes individuals who start focusing on the "soft skills"—for example, interpersonal effectiveness—can lose their drive for results. He emphasized, "Don't let this happen."

James Lindemann described the paramount importance of being open to tough feedback. He said that changing entrenched behavior sometimes requires confrontation—a very candid conversation. He also stated that this kind of feedback "is easier to hear when there is already an established relationship built upon a level of trust."[6] We tend to receive candid feedback more readily when we believe the person "is for us."

A mentor plays a key role in the success of many leaders. A mentor is a trusted advisor, who is often not our boss at the time.

Rather, a mentor is someone who understands what we do but has some experience and objectivity about the context of our position. The best mentors are often like my son's physical therapist: they are direct and go to the heart of the problem—something askew in our perspective. They are committed to our best interests even when it involves providing tough feedback.

Most senior executives I've interviewed point to the tremendous value of mentors in their own careers. Organizations often send their executives to off-site training and management development programs. While acknowledging that these programs have their place, Thomas R. Watjen stressed that the key to growing a mature executive who can handle large responsibilities in an organization is really having a mentor. Mentors typically understand the culture and the right way to get things done—how to build critical alliances to move initiatives forward.[7]

Mentors can also interpret the meaning in our circumstances. We may think we've been banished, metaphorically speaking, to outer Mongolia (no offense to outer Mongolians), but a mentor can help us recognize that everyone who gets into senior management spends a couple of years in a remote part of the business. A mentor can also explain our organization's culture and help us understand how our organization works. The key point is that for a mentor to be effective, you must be open to feedback. A mentor is not a therapist to make us *feel* better about our jobs, but is someone to challenge us to *be* better in our jobs and to explore how an improvement in our performance might happen.

Mike Volkema made an important distinction between mentors and what he called "guides." He said that a mentor is someone usually off to the side of our immediate responsibilities who we use as a sounding board and look to for advice over a long period of time. Guides usually help us on a specific project or task. We look to guides for help in managing the labyrinth of our organization for a designated problem, particularly when it has cross-functional complexity, involving multiple departments or teams.

Leaders at any level of an organization need to be particularly good at giving *and* receiving feedback. The head of leadership development of a Fortune 100 client called one morning to ask if my firm could conduct a workshop on giving and receiving feedback, with an emphasis on the receiving part. I assumed she wanted one of our trainers to lead a workshop for first-level managers. She then clarified, "I want *you* to conduct this workshop, because it's for the top thirty leaders in the company. They're the worst at giving and receiving feedback in the whole organization."

Regardless of where we might be in the organizational hierarchy, we need to develop openness to feedback. It's especially important to be open to feedback that's contradictory to how we might perceive ourselves. Our willingness to hear feedback when it suggests we're off course remains critical to making occasional mid-course corrections in order to arrive at our intended destinations.

THE HABIT OF
SELF-/OTHER-AWARENESS

In a previous chapter I stated that a lack of self-/other-awareness is Stage I of the derailment process. Because lack of self-/other-awareness is a common denominator among the derailed, the cultivation of this crucial attribute is the second habit we need to stay on track. Accurate self-awareness requires that we become a student of ourselves. It's not about falling in love with our own image in a narcissistic way, but rather that we create an accurate and balanced view of who we are and what our capabilities and limitations are.

Achieving a healthy level of self-awareness involves finding valid answers to some very important questions, such as:

- What are my strengths?
- What are my weaknesses?
- How do I come across to others?
- How do I *want* to come across to others?
- When do people respond most positively and most negatively to me?
- About what am I most passionate?
- What do I find boring and why?
- Where do I want to be in my career in three years, five years, and ten years?
- What competencies must I cultivate to arrive at those three-, five-, and ten-year destinations?
- What kind of personal brand do I want to have?
- How would others describe my personal brand?
- How do I *want* others to describe my personal brand?

The other dimension of awareness involves paying attention to others. While staying true to our own convictions is paramount, we glean tremendous insights from the reactions of others. One morning at a client's office, I sat with a marketing team during its regular weekly meeting. A member fairly new to the company talked early and often over the course of the hour-long meeting. The irritation of other team members became palpable, but "Joe" jabbered on and on. Joe and I happened to be going to the airport about the same time that afternoon, so we shared a cab. During the cab ride he asked me how I thought the idea he ventured regarding a new distribution channel for their product was received by the team.

"Joe, your idea was DOA," I said.

A bit defensively, Joe responded, "Why do you say that? That idea will make a ton of money."

"You asked me . . . do you really want to know?"

"Well, yeah."

"You talked so much in the meeting that you created resistance to your idea from the other team members. They were sending you all kinds of nonverbal signals to shut it off. You needed to listen more and not try to command so much air time."

"I don't think I said that much."

"Maybe not, but out of the ten people present, I guesstimate you spoke about 60 percent of the words uttered in the meeting."

Joe sat in stunned silence for a minute. "You know, I came from a place where dominating the conversation was the only way to get anything done. You had to overwhelm people with your ideas. The guy with the most air time usually won."

"That makes a lot of sense, but you're in a very different culture now. It's not the way to get buy-in here. I suggest you pay more attention to the nonverbal feedback you're getting from other team members."

Another person can serve as a sounding board and affords us the opportunity to test how we see ourselves and the players around us. I particularly have benefited from processing with individuals I trust when something has not gone well—i.e., learning from my mistakes.

I have a solitaire game on my PDA, and every game is winnable if you make the right moves. After I've lost a winnable game, the program includes a function that demonstrates the needed moves to win. It's always interesting to see how a critical mistake or two kept me from winning. A wise and trusted advisor serves the same role in a much more important game.

You cannot become fully aware when your own thoughts and feelings are the sole source of input. The true self also exists outside of us in the perceptions of others—this is why feedback is so valuable. Feedback from others is like a mirror that allows us to see ourselves as others do. One of the most important mirrors is people's facial expressions. There is a wealth of information in people's faces when we learn to interpret it correctly. When I coach executives, I sometimes show them photographs of people's faces and ask them to tell me how that person is feeling. "Reading others" is a critical skill.

I've heard individuals say, "I can't control what others think about me." That's a very dangerous perspective. Organizations have a brand and so do we, as individuals. Not only can we manage the perceptions of others about us, but, in an organization, we have a fundamental responsibility to do just that—it's our personal brand. It is critical that we regularly tune in to how others see us. Like a corporation, our brand is not what we say it is but rather what our "stakeholders" (manager, colleagues, direct reports, etc.) say it is. When a large gap exists between how I see myself and how others see me, it's called a blind spot. Some blind spots can derail a promising career. It's our responsibility to discover how we may be creating those perceptions and then close the gap.

We need to define what we aspire to be our personal brand and then do the market research. Here's a checklist that might be helpful as you define what you want your personal brand to convey:

- Value: In what ways do I want to add value to my team and to the product/service we provide?

- Reliability: Am I seen as someone to count on to meet deadlines and deliver a quality work product?

- Effectiveness: Am I effective in my role, and do I get the desired results?

- Collegiality: Am I easy to do business with, and do I generally get along well with others?

- Distinctiveness: Am I distinguishable from others because of the quality of my work, the follow-through, and the attention to detail?

- Positive Influence: Do I have a positive influence on others and on the process the team follows?

THE HABIT OF LISTENING TO EARLY WARNING SYSTEMS

We typically have a variety of early warning systems in our lives. My thermostat's screen told me yesterday the furnace needs a new filter. When I exercise, my heart monitor tells me when I'm getting out of training range. My car's tachometer has a red zone that warns when the engine is exceeding the safe number of RPMs for that particular engine. During his stay in the hospital, my son mentioned to me that he had ignored some warning signals before going off the jump. He was fatigued from the week of snowboarding and should have never attempted such a difficult jump in that state. He lacked the concentration and control needed to execute effectively. He didn't listen to his body.

Many great dramas deal with the consequences of ignored warning systems. One of my favorites, *A Perfect Storm*, describes the devastating consequences to a fishing boat crew and their families and friends when the crew ignores Coast Guard and other warnings to head for shore before several massive storms converge in their path.

The third habit for staying on track is to cultivate personal early warning systems that tell us when we're at risk of derailment. Personal warning systems at work vary for different individuals, but I will briefly discuss several that likely apply to most of us:

Performance Management Feedback—Pay attention to formal feedback, such as your annual appraisal. Informal feedback—for example, comments made by your boss in passing—merit special consideration. When your performance drops, it's particularly important to pay attention to how your boss interprets the problem. Your boss's indication that you dropped a ball should be a wake-up call. It's like the opening quote of this chapter . . .

making your boss nervous is going to create stress for your boss and for you.

Interpersonal Tension at Work/Low Trust Levels/Poor Communication—Conflict is a normal part of any workplace, but we should pay attention to unresolved conflict that festers. Tension with your manager or other key influencers tells you that some repair work may be needed. Conflict with colleagues or individuals in other departments may also be an important signal to heed. Similarly, when trust is low or you seem to have chronically poor communication with your manager or other key constituents, your attention should be galvanized. Pay attention to these early warning signals.

Stress—Because stress impacts our behavior so frequently and often so significantly, we will examine this early warning system in more detail.

I believe the relationship between stress and effectiveness shown in figure 3 describes how you and I *most likely* respond to stress.[8] Initially, as stress increases, our effectiveness increases as well. My father-in-law was fond of saying, "There's nothing like having a mortgage to get you out of bed and going to work every day!" When we make a presentation to our boss's leadership team, those butterflies we feel in our stomach prompt us to project more effectively and to present with more energy. As the stress level gets higher, our performance levels off. At a certain point, we then experience a precipitous drop in our performance. The "cliff" in figure 3 is a zone in which our weaknesses override our skills and capabilities, and paradoxically, we fall captive to our worst tendencies. As it increases, stress begins to impact our behavior in a decidedly negative way. We reach a point at which it's nearly impossible to mitigate stress's impact. It's like the TV commercial a few years ago about an elderly woman who falls in her home. Fortunately, she's wearing one of the special radio amulets being advertised. She presses the button to radio the medical dispatcher, and in a quivering voice, says, "I've fallen, and I can't get up." We, too, feel sometimes like we've fallen into a zone from which we cannot escape. If our stress levels get high enough, we eventually fall and can't get up.

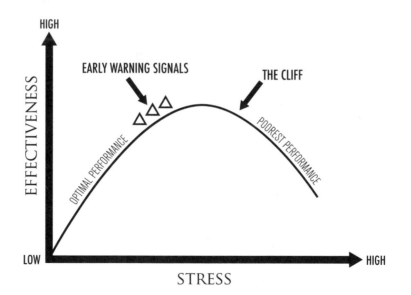

FIGURE 3

A stress early warning system gets our attention before we go off the cliff and should galvanize our focus to carefully manage our response to stress. I've actually seen leaders fail to pay attention to warning signals and lose control. In a planning meeting

I facilitated, one leader upset by his subordinates' lack of support for a new initiative he wanted to pursue, stormed out of the meeting room in an eruption of anger. His credibility with the leadership team was substantially shattered as a result of this one volatile act.

The specific warning systems that alert us to the fact that our stress level is about to "redline" varies for different individuals. For some, it's physiological, like a headache or a tense neck or fatigue. For others, it's emotional, like irritability, anger, discouragement, difficulty focusing, or lack of creativity. For me, I can always tell when a heavy travel week is starting to get to me. I start to notice my edginess. Someone talking loudly on his cell phone in a confined space like an airplane is always annoying, but when I *feel like* asking the person if he realizes how big a doofus he is, it says to me that it's time to chill. Any of these potential warning signals may indicate a need to mitigate the stress.

The key is to monitor ourselves and to pay attention to our own signals or feedback from others. Exerting control over stress means that we do whatever is necessary to lower the stress level to one at which our performance is not compromised. Noise-cancelling headphones and a good iPod playlist help me deal with Mr. Cell Phone.

The leader I described in the example above could have asked for a break. A walk in the retreat center's crisp mountain air might have helped him regain his composure *before* the damage was done. When we go too high on the stress scale, we have little to no control over what we say and do. We may want someone to rescue us, but, at work, there's no radio amulet to press.

The workplace will always be a greenhouse for stress, so the key question is, how do we mitigate it? The answer to this question must be determined individually. We need to know what raises and lowers *our* stress level while we're doing our job. "Know thyself," as Socrates opined.[9] I know some people who go to the gym during their lunch break. A midday workout may not be your thing, but I guarantee you it's better than a three-martini lunch! An extreme solution for some is to change jobs. The essential takeaway is to have an early warning system and to intervene *before* you go off the cliff.

THE HABIT OF ACCOUNTABILITY

John Donne wrote in *Meditation XVII*:

No man is an island,
Entire of itself.
Every man is a piece of the continent,
A part of the main.[10]

At work, a variety of pressures can short-circuit our thinking, causing a loss of clarity and objectivity. What's right or wrong may not be that clear-cut. We live in the shadow lands and need the clarity that so often seems to evade us in these circumstances. We're tempted to cut corners in order to make the numbers. We think about pursuing an expedient solution versus the right solution. We have real or perceived conflicts of interest. We encounter challenges to our personal or corporate values. This requires the ability to tap into the insights of people who can provide objective perspectives—individuals who know us, have our best interests in mind, and are willing to confront us with the hard facts of the situation. To find the clarity that we so desperately need, we must cultivate our sense of accountability to others, the fourth habit of the heart.

By definition, when we work in an organization, our behavior invariably impacts others. We're not islands, independent from those with whom we must work collaboratively. Patrick Lencioni drives this point home in his book *The Five Temptations of a CEO*.[11] Lencioni points out that many leaders do not foster an atmosphere in which their opinions and decisions can be challenged by others—he calls it "the desire for invulnerability." Paradoxically, vulnerability on the part of a leader raises trust and respect. Lencioni says that leaders need to be accountable to others through having their views refined in the fire of productive conflict.

The leaders most susceptible to derailment refuse to have their opinions, decisions, and actions questioned. Insularity contributes significantly to derailment. Accountability means that, even if we're not required to answer to others because of our position or corporate policy or law, we intentionally place ourselves in relationship with someone who tests our motives and our actions.

Leaders can't ask permission for most decisions. They're paid to make decisions, but when it involves a conflict of interest, such as personal benefit, accountability to others raises the integrity of our decisions. Would Tyco's CEO Dennis Kowalski have spent six thousand dollars on a shower curtain for his Manhattan apartment with company money if he had run that questionable decision past a reasonable person or two? Would Merrill Lynch's chairman and CEO John Thain have spent over a million dollars redecorating his private office during a period in which Merrill Lynch's stockholders lost billions if he had asked an objective and trusted colleague if it was the best time to spruce up his digs? These decisions don't pass the "smell test" that a reasonable and objective person would apply.

Many leaders have a need for power and control, which is normal for someone willing to stand at the helm of a large and complex organization. Healthy, effective leaders also appreciate and respect others. A leader with a high need for power and control and a low appreciation of others was reflected in the style of Home Depot's former CEO Bob Nardelli, who failed to gain the alignment of the people who actually did the work. In contrast, Richard Anderson, CEO of Delta Air Lines, points out, "You've got to be thankful to the people who get the work done." He handwrites half a dozen thank-you notes a day to Delta employees.[12]

In some leaders the appreciation *for* others can morph into a need to be appreciated *by* others. The excessive need for the approval of others predisposes a leader to make a popular decision versus the harder right decision. Accountability means we are willing to have our decisions questioned, but we're not conducting daily tracking polls with fellow leaders trying to make the most popular decision. Self-aware leaders pay attention to their own need for the approval of others any time they make a significant decision.

We are usually accountable to a manager, a team, or a board to achieve the stated objectives of our jobs. We need to keep our commitments, to take ownership of our assignments, and to pursue excellence in every aspect of our jobs. This responsibility to others should have a galvanizing effect on our behavior at work. A failure to be accountable leads to derailment.

THE HABIT OF RESILIENCY

Golf is incredibly addictive. It is a perfect illustration of what psychologists call a "variable ratio of reinforcement." In non-textbook jargon, that means, in a given round, we hit enough good shots to keep us coming back. There are few things in life as satisfying as crushing a drive, followed by a perfect 7-iron shot to the green a few feet from the pin and then making a five-foot putt for a birdie. This scenario doesn't happen that often for me, but when it does, I begin to wonder, *Maybe I should consider trying to get my card for the senior tour . . .*

Several years ago I attended a PGA event held on a course where I play often. I discovered that there are only a few differences between the pros and me—but the differences are really important. First, they hit a lot more great shots than I do. Oddly enough, as I followed some of the greatest players in the world, I noted that they made the very same mistakes I do, such as landing an approach shot in a bunker. There are two critical differences, though, in how they handle those mistakes. First, they are a lot better at getting out of trouble than I am. Second, they don't let mistakes or bad luck get in their psyches, as I seem to do. When I hit a shot into the woods, it takes me another hole or two to get over it. The pros make a bad shot, get frustrated, and get over it before they hit another. They are resilient. To stay on track, we must develop the fifth habit of the heart—resiliency.

When bad things happen to us, it's tempting to stew in our own emotional juices—to be the victim. I get that. I'm quite skilled at bringing the past into the present and then dragging the present into the future. When I read books about bad things happening to good people, I naturally identify with the good person in the story. *I'm a good person—why are all these bad things happening to me?*

Resilience is about snapping back. It's about getting up and keeping going. Resilient people deal with setbacks more effectively. They handle adversity better. The resilient people I know still get frustrated, but they somehow don't carry that frustration into the future. I rarely hear effective leaders use hackneyed clichés, such as, "When the going gets tough, the tough get going." Their resolve seems to come from deeper convictions about life and work. They have an inner confidence that says, *We will get through this. We will not be thwarted by these circumstances.*

Resilience is the ability not only to bounce back from adversity but also to grow from it. The most successful business leaders encounter challenges, recover from them, and become stronger, more capable leaders and more developed people because of them. Powerful and relevant examples of this principle are the U.S. soldiers who experience combat. Army doctors have found that while some soldiers interpret combat as traumatic and suffer post-traumatic stress disorder as a result (this has been widely publicized in recent years), those who are resilient recover from their experiences and grow into stronger, more confident leaders and people.

I don't know anyone who relishes adversity, but I do know individuals who believe that they've been made stronger through it. The first-century writer Paul expressed this thought when he said, "We also exult in our tribulations, knowing that tribulation brings about perseverance; and perseverance, proven character; and proven character, hope."[13]

Research demonstrates that a critical factor in a person's

resilience is the people in their lives. Personal and professional networks provide support, guidance, perspective, and new opportunities in the midst of challenging setbacks. A crucial action we can take to strengthen our resilience is to cultivate relationships within our family, our company, our profession, and our community.

Perhaps the most important contributor to resilience is clarity of purpose. Developing a clear sense of purpose gives meaning and context to our work and widens our perspective in our jobs. While we want to know that we are being paid fairly, we will almost always work harder for meaning than we will for money. Meaning also helps us persevere.

My favorite series of TV commercials in recent years are the Boeing ads called "That's Why We're Here." These skillfully crafted, short commercials depict a series of various Boeing products and technologies employed in various commercial, military, and humanitarian settings. Many different roles in the organization are depicted, such as engineers, project managers, and administrative personnel. "That's why we're here" connects the people of Boeing to the beneficiaries of their work. For example, soldiers are protected by their technology and the victims of natural disasters receive relief supplies because of Boeing's powerful aircraft. We need "that's why we're here" clarity to find meaning in our jobs and ultimately to be resilient.[14]

Leaders who want to bring out the best in the individuals they lead will pay particular attention to this powerful principle. We want those we lead to do more than just show up for work. We want them to gain an emotional commitment to their jobs. Meaning is what fuels the ownership we want our employees to experience in their work. Also, given the dramatic changes that many organizations have experienced recently, those we lead can tolerate a lot of adversity when they know that the value of their jobs transcends the turbulence we experience at a given moment.

MAKING THE HABITS OUR OWN

These five critical habits of the heart reflect the disciplines we must employ to stay on track. For these disciplines to become a part of who we are, we must do them intentionally. The payoff is becoming the person and the worker we each want to be.

EPILOGUE

It is my hope that this book and the additional materials available on the book's Web site (www.derailedleader.com) will be useful resources that provide you with significant insight into who you are and how to be a person who stays on track. We need eight gigawatts of insight to be effective in today's workplace. The derailment risk assessment is a free tool available on the Web site that provides feedback and developmental recommendations. We must keep intense light on our character as well as continue to become more and more competent at what we do.

My sincere wish is that *Derailed* will be as meaningful for you to read as it has been for me to write. After the release of my earlier book, *Run with the Bulls Without Getting Trampled,* many wrote letters or e-mailed me with their comments, reactions, appreciations, and hopes. I look forward to hearing from you as well.

NOTES

Derailed

1. George Will, "Shock of Recognition," Newsweek, 25 July 1977, 80.
2. Michael Blood, "NTSB to Seek Cell Phone Records in LA Train Crash," Associated Press, 14 September 2008. Available at http://abcnews.go.com/US/wireStory?id=5797635. Daisy Nguyen, "Train engineer texted 22 seconds before LA crash," Associated Press Newswires, 2 October 2008.
3. Matt Kempner, "Nardelli out at Home Depot: New CEO brings new tone." The Atlanta Journal-Constitution, 4 January 2007, C1.
4. Paul J. Brouwer, "The Power to See Ourselves," Harvard Business Review, November–December 1964.
5. "Harvard's Lessons in Management; Summers' provocative style may push his lofty goals out of reach," BusinessWeek, editorial, 7 March 2005.
6. Patricia Sellers and Cora Daniels, "The 50 Most Powerful Women in American Business," Fortune #138, no. 7, 12 October 1998. Fiorina achieved the number one position on this ranking for six years, beginning in 1998. See also Fortune issues on 25 October 1999, 16 October 2000, 15 October 2001, 14 October 2002, and 13 October 2003.
7. Shakespeare, Macbeth, act 1, scene 7, 26–28.
8. Peter F. Drucker, "Making Strength Productive, The Effective Executive" in The Effective Executive, (New York: Harper & Row Publishers, 1966), 95.
9. Pat MacMillan, Performance Factor (Nashville: Broadman & Holman Publishers, 2001), 4.

10. A. Shoshaman A Tale of Corporate Japan, The BlackCoat.com, 11 Nov 2006.

11. K. Auletta, "The Lost Tycoon," New Yorker, 23 April 2001.

PROFILE #1: BOB NARDELLI

1. Patricia Seller, "Something to prove Bob Nardelli was stunned when Jack Welch told him he'd never run GE. 'I want an autopsy!' he demanded," Fortune 24 June 2002, http://money.cnn.com/magazines/fortune/fortune_archive/2002/06/24/325190/index.htm.

2. Ibid.

3. Ibid.

4. Seller, "Something to Prove Bob Nardelli was stunned."

5. Ibid.

6. Ibid.

7. Background provided on Charlie Rose.com of Guest Bob Nardelli prior to 20 July 2004, interview. http://www.charlierose.com/guest/view/1421.

8. Victoria Griffith, "Winning Hearts and Minds at Home Depot," Strategy & Business, Spring 2005.

9. "Robert L. Nardelli, 1948–," http://www.referenceforbusiness.com/biography/M-R/Nardelli-Robert-L-1948.html.

10. Patricia Sellers, "Exit the Builder, Enter the Repairman: Home Depot's Arthur Blank Is Out. New CEO Bob Nardelli Is In. His Job: To Tackle the Company's Renovation After Two Decades of Nonstop Expansion," Fortune, 19 March 2001, 86–88.

11. Griffith, "Winning Hearts and Minds at Home Depot."

12. Ibid.

13. Bruce Nussbaum, "Lessons from Home Depot's Bob Nardelli—Why Command and Control Is So Bad," BusinessWeek/Nussbaum on Design Post, January 2004, http://www.business-week.com/innovate/NussbaumOnDesign/archives/2007/01/lessons_from_ho.html.

14. "The Fixer-Upper: The Former GE Exec Is Finally Getting Credit for Doing the Kind of Bold Renovations at Home Depot That the No. 2 U.S. Retailer Promotes Among Do-It-Yourselfers," Institutional Investor, January 2004, 18–19.

15. Brian Grow, "Out at Home Depot," BusinessWeek, 15 January 2007. http://www.businessweek.com/magazine/content/07_03/b4017001.htm.

16. Jennifer Pellet, "Mr. Fix-It Steps In," Chief Executive, October 2001, 44–47.

17. http://www.businessweek.com/magazine/content/07_03/b3974001.htm.

18. Julie Creswell and Michael Barboro, "Home Depot Ousts Highly Paid Chief," New York Times, 4 January 2007. http://www.nytimes.com/2007/01/04/business/04home.html?pagewanted=print.

19. Dale Buss, "Risky Business," Forbes.com, 26 March 2008. http://www.forbes.com/2008/03/26/buss-ceos-image-lead-manage-cx_db_0326reputation.html.

20. Dean Foust, "What Worked at GE Isn't Working at Home Depot," BusinessWeek News & Commentary, with Brian Grow in Ocala, Florida, 27 January 2003. http://www.businessweek.com/magazine/content/03_04/b3817076.htm.

21. Nussbaum, "Lessons from Home Depot's Bob Nardelli."

22. Grow, "Out at Home Depot."

23. "What's Ahead? Home Depot's new chairman and chief executive, Frank Blake, will get a chance to test his diplomatic skills in several areas," Atlanta Journal Constitution, 5 January 2007.

24. Knowledge@Wharton, "Home Unimprovement: Was Nardelli's Tenure at Home Depot a Blueprint for Failure?" 10 January 2007, http://knowledge.wharton.upenn.edu/article.cfm?articleid=1636.

25. Home Depot Inc Annual Shareholders Meeting – Final. Fair Disclosure Wire Publication Date: 25 May 2006, http://www.accessmylibrary.com/coms2/summary_0286-15544562_ITM?email=acemarriott@gmail.com&library.

26. Knowledge@Wharton, "Home Unimprovement."

27. Home Depot Inc Annual Shareholders Meeting – Final. Fair Disclosure.

28. Grow, "Out at Home Depot."

29. Heidi N. Moore, "Chrysler: The End of Bob Nardelli. Again," Deal Journal, April 21, 2009, http://blogs.wsj.com/deals/2009/04/21/chrysler-the-end-of-bob-nardelli-again/.

PROFILE #2: CARLY FIORINA

1. Louise Kehoe, "Fiorina Moves to Put Hewlett-Packard Back Together," Financial Times, 7 December 1999.

2. Peter Burrows, "HP's Carly Fiorina: The Boss," BusinessWeek, 2 August 1999. Available at http://www.businessweek.com/1999/99_31/b3640003.htm.

3. "Two Close-Ups of HP's Carly Fiorina" (book review), BusinessWeek, February 17, 2003. Available at http://www.businessweek.com/magazine/content/03_07/b3820037_mz005.htm.

4. Ibid.

5. Ibid.

6. George Anders, "The Carly Chronicles: An Inside Look at Her Campaign to Reinvent HP," Fast Company, 1 February 2003.

7. "What's News," Wall Street Journal, 20 July 1999, Business and Finance.

8. Louise Kehoe, "Fiorina Moves to Put Hewlett-Packard Back Together," Financial Times, 7 December 1999.

9. Ibid.

10. Bill Saporito, et. al, "Why Carly's Out: HP's ousted CEO, Carly Fiorina, tried to revive the Silicon Valley legend with the vision thing. What the company needs is far more fundamental," Time, 21 February 2005.

11. Pui-Wing Tam, "Hewlett-Packard Board Considers a Reorganization—Management Moves Stem from Performance Concerns; Helping Fiorina 'Succeed,'" Wall Street Journal, 24 January 2005.

12. Saporito, "Why Carly's Out."

13. Ben Elgin, "The Inside Story of Carly's Ouster," BusinessWeek, 21 February 2005.

14. Pui-Wing Tam, "Fallen Star: H-P's Board Ousts Fiorina as CEO—Amid Languishing Stock, Computer Chief Resists Pressure to Delegate—A Big Merger's Missed Goals," Wall Street Journal, 10 February 2005.

15. Elgin, "The Inside Story of Carly's Ouster."

16. Saporito, "Why Carly's Out."

17. Paul R. La Monica, "Fiorina Out, HP Stock Soars," CNNMoney.com, February 10, 2005. Available at http://money.cnn.com/2005/02/09/technology/hp_fiorina/index.htm.

18. Tam, "Fallen Star."

19. Saporito, "Why Carly's Out."

20. Tam, "Fallen Star."

21. George Anders, Perfect Enough: Carly Fiorina and the Reinvention of Hewlett-Packard (New York: Portfolio, 2003), 211.

22. Peter Burrows, "The Radical: Carly Fiorina's Bold Management Experiment at HP," BusinessWeek, 19 February 2001. Available at http://www.businessweek.com/archives/2001/b3720001.arc.htm.

23. Peter Burrows, Backfire: Carly Fiorina's High-Stakes Battle for the Soul of Hewlett-Packard (Hoboken, NJ:John Wiley & Sons, 2003), 261–62.

24. Burrows, "The Radical."

25. Tam, "Fallen Star."

26. Carly Fiorina, Tough Choices (New York: Portfolio Trade, 2007), 236–37.

27. Ibid.

28. Ray Tiernan, "A Memoir with Much Reflection, Little Depth— Fiorina admits to few mistakes—beyond a too trusting nature— in her fiery downfall at HP," ed., Jay Palmer, Barron's, 6 November 2006.

PROFILE #3: DURK JAGER #3

1. David Bennady, "Culture Vulture," Marketing Week, 17 September 1998. Richard Tomkins, "Procter & Gamble Banks on Two Chiefs: Consumer products giant hopes to combine the talents of a popular team player and a hard-nosed decision maker," Financial Post (London), 25 March 1995.

2. Robert Berner, "P&G New and Improved: How A. G. Lafley is revolutionizing a bastion of corporate conservatism," BusinessWeek, 7 July 2003.

3. Katrina Brooker, "Can Procter & Gamble Change Its Culture, Protect Its Market Share, and Find the Next Tide?"26 April 1999, http://money.cnn.com/magazines/fortune/fortune_archive/1999/04/26/258788/index.htm.

4. Patrick Larkin, "Hard-driving Jager Launches New P&G," Cincinnati Post, 10 September 1998, 1A.

5. "Harvard's Lessons in Management.

6. Brooker, "Can Procter & Gamble Change Its Culture?"

7. David Bennady, "Culture Vulture," Marketing Week, 17 September 1998.

8. Brooker, "Can Procter & Gamble Change Its Culture?"

9. "Procter & Gamble—Jager's Gamble," The Economist, 30 October 1999.

10. Brooker, "Can Procter & Gamble Change Its Culture?"

11. Berner, "P&G New and Improved."

12. Ibid.

13. Daniel Eisenberg and Daren Fonda, "A Healthy Gamble: How did A. G. Lafley turn Procter & Gamble's old brands into hot items? Here's the beauty of it," Time, 16 September 2002.

14. Ibid.

15. Berner, "P&G New and Improved."

16. Bennady, "Culture Vulture."

17. Brooker, "Can Procter & Gamble Change Its Culture?"

18. Ibid.

19. John A. Byrne, "Leaders Are Made, Not Born," BusinessWeek, 17 February 2003.

20. Warren G. Bennis and Robert J. Thomas, Geeks and Geezers: How Eras, Values, and Defining Moments Shape Leaders, (Harvard Business Press, 2002), 134.

21. David Leonhardt, "Procter & Gamble Shake-Up Follows Poor Profit Outlook," New York Times, 9 June 2000.

PROFILE #4: STEVEN HEYER

1. Alan Murray, "Starwood's Early-Checkout Mystery," Wall Street Journal, 11 April 2007.

2. Marcus Baram, "Misconduct in the Corner Office," April 11, 2007, http://abcnews.go.com/Business/Story?id=3027563&page=1.

3. Robyn Taylor Parets, "New Starwood CEO to Add Fizz?" National Real Estate Investor, 1 November 2004.

4. "Starwood Hotels & Resorts Names Steven J. Heyer Chief Executive Officer," Hospitality.net, 21 September 2004.

5. David Goetzl, "Maverick Marketer Steve Heyer out as Starwood CEO," Media Daily News, 3 April 2007.

6. Evelyn M. Rusli, "Heyer Checks Out of Starwood," Forbes.com, 3 April 2007.

7. Ibid.

8. Peter Sanders and Joann S. Lublin, "Starwood CEO's Ouster Followed Battle with Board over His Conduct," Wall Street Journal, 7 April 2007.

9. Ibid.

10. Rusli, "Heyer Checks Out of Starwood."

11. Baram, "Misconduct in the Corner Office."

12. Sanders and Lublin, "Starwood CEO's Ouster Followed Battle with Board over His Conduct."

13. Ibid.

14. Ibid.

15. Oliver Staley and Amy Wilson, "Starwood Chief Heyer Quits, Fueling Takeover Talk," ehotelier.com, 3 April 2007.

16. Murray, "Starwood's Early-Checkout Mystery."

17. Emily Chasan, "Starwood CEO's meager pay-off puzzles Wall Street," Reuters, 2 April 2007.

18. Rusli, "Heyer Checks Out of Starwood."

19. Ibid.

PROFILE #5: FRANK RAINES

1. Eric Dash, "A Whistle-Blower Is Kept in the Wings at the Hearing," New York Times, 7 October 2004.

2. Richard W. Stevenson, "A Homecoming at Fannie Mae; Franklin Raines Takes Charge of a Most Political Company," New York Times, 17 May 1998.

3. Ibid.

4. Laura Cohn, "Protecting Fannie's Franchise," BusinessWeek, 9 December 2002.

5. Stevenson, "A Homecoming at Fannie Mae."

6. David Bogoslaw with Ben Steverman, John Cady, and Will Andrews "Key Figures in the Financial Crisis," BusinessWeek, 18 October 2008.

7. http://en.wikipedia.org/wiki/Franklin_Raines#cite_note-14.

8. Cohn, "Protecting Fannie's Franchise."

9. www.wnd.com/index.php?fa=PAGE.view&pageId=75802.

10. www.kmblegal.com/cases_oct_07_04.php.

11. Ibid.

12. Ibid.

13. Terence O'Hara, "Accountant Says Fannie Mae Pressured Him— Barnes's Statement to House Panel Alleges Retaliation for His Objections," Washington Post, 7 October 2004. http://www. washingtonpost.com/wp-dyn/articles/A13346-2004Oct6.html.

14. Stephen Labaton, "Fannie Mae Crisis Raises Concerns on Leadership," New York Times, 29 September 2004.

15. Patricia O'Connell, ed., "Frank Raines Takes on the Critics," BusinessWeek Online Extra, 30 June 2003.

16. Testimony by Franklin D. Raines Before the House Subcommittee on Capital Markets, Insurance and Government, Sponsored Enterprises (Written Testimony), Washington, DC, 6 October 2004.

17. Stephen Labaton, "Chief Says Fannie Mae Did Nothing Wrong," New York Times, 7 October 2004.

18. http://www.wnd.com/index.php?fa=PAGE.view&pageId=75802.

19. Associated Press, "Bio Box for Franklin Delano Raines," Los Angeles Times, 30 December 2004.

20. Dash, "A Whistle-Blower Is Kept in the Wings at the Hearing."

21. Mike McNamee, "Franklin Raines's Lost Gamble," BusinessWeek, 22 December 2004.

22. "Fannie Mae Liberals," Wall Street Journal, 14 October 2004.

23. McNamee, "Franklin Raines's Lost Gamble."

24. "Culprits of the Collapse," Anderson 360 story, CNN aired 23 October 2008.

PROFILE #6: DICK FULD

1. Tom Bawden, "Bruiser of Wall St. Dick Fuld looked after his people, but didn't know when to quit," Times Online, 16 September 2008.

2. Ibid.

3. Alice Gomstyn, "Bleeding Green: The Fall of Fuld," ABC News, 6 October 2008, http://abcnews.go.com/Business/Economy/story?id=5951669&page=1.

4. Ibid.

5. Ibid.

6. Steve Fishman, "Burning Down His House," New York, 30 November 2008.

7. Gomstyn, "Bleeding Green."

8. Suzanne Craig, et al, "The Weekend That Wall Street Died—Ties That Long United Strongest Firms Unraveled as Lehman Sank Toward Failure," Wall Street Journal, 29 December 2008.

9. Fishman, "Burning Down His House."

10. Mark DeCambre, "GE Unplugged Fuld," New York Post, 25 September 2008.

11. Tom Bawden, "Bruiser of Wall St Dick Fuld looked after his people, but didn't know when to quit," Times Online, 16 September 2008.

12. Gomstyn, "Bleeding Green."

13. C-SPAN, "Bankruptcy of Lehman Brothers Testimony by Dick Fuld," House Oversight and Government Reform Committee, 6 October 2008.

14. John Gapper, "A Tragedy of Hubris and Nemesis," Financial Times, 14 September 2008.

DERAILMENT IS A PROCESS

1. Proverbs 16:18 (The Message).

2. Stephen J. Spignesi, The 100 Greatest Disasters of All Time (Citadel, 2002).

3. Britannica Online Encyclopedia, "Bihar train disaster," http://www.britannica.com/EBchecked/topic/1481326/Bihar-train-disaster.

4. Steve McShane, Currents, Organizational Behavior Developments in Research and Practice, March 2007.

5. Martha Lagace, Gerstner: Changing Culture at IBM—Lou Gerstner Discusses Changing the Culture at IBM, Working Knowledge, 9 December 2002, http://hbswk.hbs.edu/archive/3209.html.

6. Lou Gerstner, Who Says Elephants Can't Dance? Inside IBM's Historic Turnaround (New York: Harper Collins, 2002), Dedication.

7. Jim Collins, How the Mighty Fall and Why Some Companies Never Give In (New York: Harper Collins, 2009), 162.

8. Elgin, "The Inside Story of Carly's Ouster."

WHAT'S YOUR CHARACTER QUOTIENT?

1. Jeffrey Toobin, The Run of His Life: The People v. O. J. Simpson (New York: Simon & Schuster, 1997), 58.

2. Os Guinness, Character Counts (Grand Rapids: Baker Books, 1999).

3. David Gergen, "Character vs. Capacity," U.S. News & World Report, 22 October 2000, http://www.usnews.com/usnews/opinion/articles/001030/archive_010452.htm.

4. Bret Stephens, "Celebrity Culture vs. The Right Stuff," Wall Street Journal, 21 July 2009.

5. Os Guinness, When No One Sees: The Importance of Character in an Age of Image (Colorado Springs: NavPress Publishing Group, 2000), 16.

6. Anthony Hopkins as Charles Morse in The Edge (1997), directed by Lee Tamahori, screenplay by David Mamet. Available at http://www.youtube.com/watch?v=EWRmXbxeuUk.

THE REAL DEAL

1. William Shakespeare, Macbeth, act 1, scene 7, line 83.

2. WordNet, Princeton University, 2006.

3. Gergen, "Character vs. Capacity."

4. James M. Kouzes and Barry Z. Posner, Credibility (San Francisco: Jossey-Bass, 1993).

5. John Powell, Why Am I Afraid to Tell You Who I Am? Insights into Personal Growth (Chicago: Thomas More Association, 1995).

6. Flannery O'Connor, A Good Man Is Hard to Find and Other Stories (Harcourt, 1992).

GET AHOLD OF YOURSELF

1. Warner Mack, "Bridge Washed Out," http://www.kovideo.net/lyrics/w/Warner-Mack/Bridge-Washed-Out.html.

2. Daniel Goleman, "What Makes a Leader?" Harvard Business Review, January 2004.

3. D. Goeman, R. Boyatzis, A. McKee, Primal Leadership (Boston: Harvard Business School Press, 2002).

4. Personal interview with James Lindemann, May 12, 2009.

THE STAR OF YOUR OWN SHOW

1. Robert Slater, The GE Way Fieldbook. Jack Welch's Battle Plan for Corporate Revolution (New York: McGraw Hill, 2000), 21.

2. Arthur Levitt Jr., "The Imperial CEO Is No More," Wall Street Journal, 17 March 2005.

3. Jim Collins, Good to Great (New York: Harper Business, 2001), 21.

4. Ibid., 27.

5. Personal interview with Patrick Gelsinger, May 25, 2009.

6. Personal interview with Michael Volkema, May 26, 2009.

7. Stephen R. Covey, The 8th Habit: From Effectiveness to Greatness (New York: Free Press, 2004), 300.

8. Levitt, "The Imperial CEO Is No More."

9. Personal interview with Lindemann, May 12, 2009.

10. Telephone interview with Mike Volkema, May 26, 2009.

AN AMAZING ORDINARY HERO

1. Open Range, starring Kevin Costner and Robert Duval, 2003, http://www.imdb.com/title/tt0316356/.

2. Atlanta Journal, Vol. 84, No. 228, November 19, 1966, 1.

3. Open Range.

4. Plato, The Apology of Socrates, Phaedo and Crito (Harvard Classics, available online at http://www.bartleby.com/2/1/1.html).

5. Carl Olof Cederlund, Vasa I: The Archaeology of a Swedish Warship of 1628, ed. Fred Hocker (Statens Maritima Museer [National Maritime Museum of Sweden], 2006).

6. E. Fairley, "Why the Vasa Sank: 10 Lessons Learned" (Oregon professor paper based on research of original sources, available at http://faculty.up.edu/lulay/failure/vasacasestudy.pdf).

7. Web site of Vasamuseet, the Vasa Museum in Stockholm, Sweden. See http://www.vasamuseet.se/InEnglish/about.aspx.

8. Martin Seligman, Penn Positive Psychology Center Abstract, 2007.

9. Robert P. Miles, Warren Buffett Wealth (Hoboken, NJ: John Wiley & Sons, 2004), 157.

HABITS OF THE HEART TO STAY ON TRACK

1. William Oncken Jr., Managing Management Time, (Englewood Cliffs: Prentice Hall, Inc., 1984): 238. www.onchencorp.com.

2. Personal interview with Thomas R. Watjen, May 13, 2009.

3. Personal interview with Patrick P. Gelsinger, May 26, 2009.

4. Personal interview with Michael A. Volkema, May 25, 2009.

5. Adapted from Cynthia D. McCauley, Russ S. Moxley, and Ellen Van Velsor, "Top Ten Reasons for Rejecting Your 360-Degree Feedback," in The Center for Creative Leadership Handbook of Leadership Development, 1st ed. (San Francisco: Jossey-Bass, 1998), 49.

6. Personal interview with James Lindemann, May 12, 2009.

7. Personal interview with Thomas R. Watjen, May 13, 2009 .

8. Some research contradicts what scientists call a curvilinear relationship between stress and effectiveness shown in Figure 1. The scientific debate has gone on since the early 1900s. Some findings indicate that any stress compromises effectiveness—a negative linear relationship. Intuitively, Figure 1 describes what we often experience, so I present this as a model vs. a scientifically based conclusion.

9. John Barlett's Familiar Quotations, 10th ed., 1919, quotes a reference to this saying by Plutarch. According to Barlett, Plutarch ascribes the saying to Plato, though it is "also ascribed to Pythagoras, Chilo, Thales, Cleobulus, Bias, and Socrates, as well as Phemone, a mythical Greek poetess of the ante-Homeric period. Juvenal (Satire xi. 27) says that this precept descended from heaven."

10. John Donne, For Whom the Bell Tolls. This passage was originally written by Donne not as a poem but as prose. It comes from

Meditation XVII of his 1624 Devotions upon Emergent Occasions, which is available in full text via Project Gutenberg at http://www.gutenberg.org/files/23772/23772-8.txt. The original quote is, "No man is an island, entire of itself; every man is a piece of the continent, a part of the main."

11. Patrick Lencioni, The Five Temptations of a CEO: A Leadership Fable (San Francisco: Jossey-Bass, 1998).

12. Adam Bryant, "He Wants Subjects, Verbs and Objects," The New York Times, 26 April 2009.

13. Romans 5:3–4 (New American Standard Bible).

14. Boeing commercial, "That's Why We're Here," http://www.youtube.com/watch?v=ot2uCKr5OZA&NR=1

ACKNOWLEDGMENTS

Although one author's name is listed on the front of this book, many have contributed to this effort. Most of all, I want to thank my dear wife, Anne, whose encouragement to persist in this new venture of writing has made all the difference! I also want to thank my clients, from whom I've learned so much over the years. They exemplify competence and character. Many thanks to my agent, Robert Wolgemuth, and his team, who excel at author representation, and they have also mastered the art of encouragement. I want to thank my close friend and professional colleague, Pat MacMillan, without whose many hours of white-board sessions, generosity with ideas, and feedback on drafts of the manuscript, this book would not have come to pass. My two brilliant MBA research assistants, Richard Marriott and Elisabeth Irwin, masterfully sought out the needed background information for the six leader profiles and helped integrate their findings into the book. My new publisher, Joel Miller, enthusiastically embraced this book and has been a huge supporter of the importance of its message. My new editor, Kristen Parrish, has been tremendously insightful about how best to organize this book and how to tell the story. My managing editor, Heather Skelton, skillfully and graciously shepherded the project to completion. I also want to thank my longtime colleague and friend, Dr. Gail Wise, who created the individual web-based assessment that complements this book. Additionally, I want to thank four senior leaders who contributed their insight about the derailment process and how emerging leaders can stay on track:

PATRICK P. GELSINGER
Senior Vice President,
Intel Corporation

JAMES J. LINDEMANN,
President and Chief Executive Officer,
Emerson Motor Company

MICHAEL A. VOLKEMA
Chairman of the Board and former Chief Executive Officer,
Herman Miller, Inc.

THOMAS R. WATJEN
President and Chief Executive Officer,
Unum Group

ABOUT THE AUTHOR

Timothy Irwin, Ph.D., has consulted with many of America's most well-respected organizations and top *Fortune 100* companies for more than twenty years. He also served in a senior management post for a U.S.-based company with more than three hundred offices worldwide. He is a frequent speaker on leadership development, organizational effectiveness, and executive selection. Presently, he is managing partner of IrwinInc, psychologists to business.

INDEX

Stay On Track with Online Resources

→ Take a FREE Derailed Assessment to Help You Avoid Derailment

→ Sign Up for Dr. Tim Irwin's FREE Newsletter

→ Access FREE Downloadable Tools

→ Access FREE Audio and Video Resources

→ ... AND MORE!

Go to www.DerailedLeader.com to download your FREE resources.

About the Author

Tim Irwin, Ph.D., is an author, speaker, and leading authority on leadership development, organizational effectiveness, and executive selection. For more than twenty years, he has consulted with many of America's most well-respected organizations and top Fortune 100 companies.

Tim has assisted corporations in diverse industries, including fiber optics, real estate, financial services, baby products, information technologies, news and entertainment, insurance, hotels, high-technology research, chemicals, floor covering, bottling, quick service restaurants, fibers and textiles, electronics, and pharmaceuticals. He served for a number of years as the facilitator of the Regional Leadership Institute in Atlanta. His work has taken him to more than twenty-five countries in Europe, Latin America, Canada, and Asia.

Tim worked from 2000 to 2005 in senior management for a firm with more than 300 offices worldwide, specializing in organizational effectiveness, talent management, and leadership development. He has served on both for-profit and non-profit boards and is currently managing partner of IrwinInc.

Tim received his A.B. and M.A. degrees from the University of Georgia in Athens. His Ph.D. training included a dual major in industrial/organizational and clinical psychology from Georgia State University in Atlanta. He is a licensed psychologist and an adjunct professor of psychology at the University of Georgia and the Reformed Theological Seminary in Orlando, Florida.

To contact Dr. Tim Irwin go to or www.DrTimIrwin.com.

Speaking

Drawing from more than twenty years as a corporate psychologist who has consulted with, interviewed, and studied thousands of high performing individuals, executives, and teams. He shares practical insights and strategies to help you and your team avoid Derailment and stay on track.

Tim speaks frequently on leadership development, employee engagement, organizational effectiveness, and executive selection. From one-on-one's with CEOs and key business leaders to executive roundtables, management sessions, and large conference events, Dr. Irwin's combination of practical insight and masterful storytelling enable him to connect with an audience and impart knowledge that leads to results.

Are you ready to Run with the Bulls?

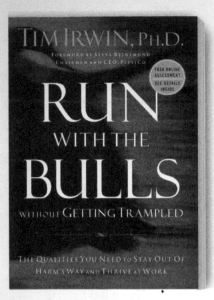

Dr. Tim Irwin is also the author of *Run with the Bulls without Getting Trampled: The Qualities You Need to Stay Out of Harms Way* and T*hrive at Work*. Learn more about *Run with the Bulls*, take a FREE online assessment and find development resources, at **www.RunwiththeBulls.net**

Double the Impact with *Run with the Bulls* and *Derailed* Together!

Books are available to order online and where most books are sold.

For bulk orders, visit your local retailer, contact Thomas Nelson Publishers specialty sales, or email Bulk@DrTimIrwin.com.